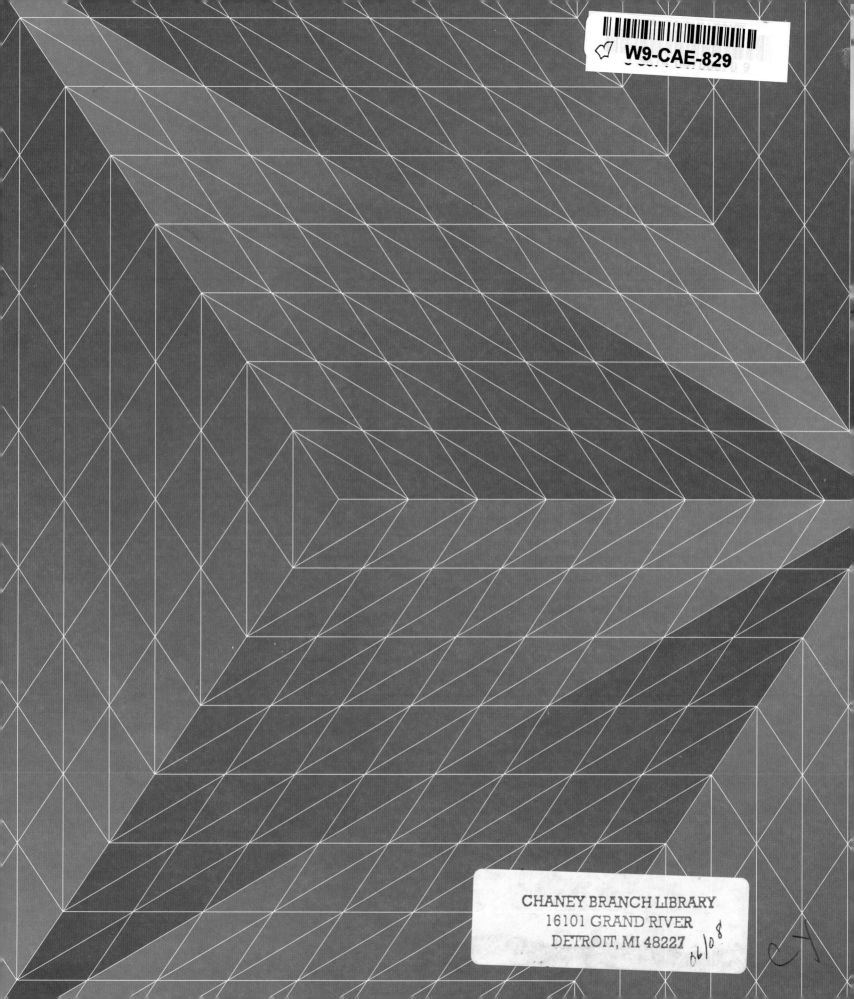

Human Body

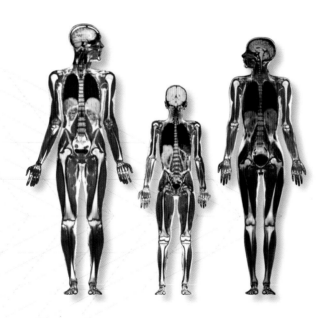

SIMON & SCHUSTER BOOKS FOR YOUNG READERS
An imprint of Simon & Schuster Children's Publishing Division
1230 Avenue of the Americas, New York, New York 10020

Conceived and produced by Weldon Owen Pty Ltd
61 Victoria Street, McMahons Point
Sydney, NSW 2060, Australia

Group Chief Executive Officer John Owen
President and Chief Executive Officer Terry Newell
Publisher Sheena Coupe
Creative Director Sue Burk
Concept Development John Bull, The Book Design Company
Editorial Coordinator Mike Crowton
Vice President, International Sales Stuart Laurence
Vice President, Sales and New Business Development Amy Kaneko
Vice President, Sales: Asia and Latin America Dawn Low
Administrator, International Sales Kristine Ravn

Project Editor Helen Flint
Illustrations* and Design Argosy Publishing, www.argosypublishing.com ARGOSY
Cover Designers Gaye Allen and Kelly Booth

Color reproduction by Chroma Graphics (Overseas) Pte Ltd
Printed by SNP Leefung Printers Ltd
Manufactured in China

A WELDON OWEN PRODUCTION
SIMON & SCHUSTER BOOKS FOR YOUNG READERS is a trademark of Simon & Schuster, Inc.
The text for this book is set in Meta and Rotis Serif.
10 9 8 7 6 5 4 3 2

Library of Congress Cataloging-in-Publication Data
Calabresi, Linda.
Human body / Linda Calabresi.
p. cm. — (Insiders)

ISBN-13: 978-1-4169-3861-3 (Hardcover)
ISBN-10: 1-4169-3861-3 (Hardcover)

1. Human physiology—Juvenile literature. 2. Body, Human—Juvenile literature. I. Title.
QP37.C315 2007
612—dc22
2007061744

* With the exception of some additional illustrations. See page 64 for details.

Human Body

Linda Calabresi

Simon & Schuster Books for Young Readers
New York London Toronto Sydney

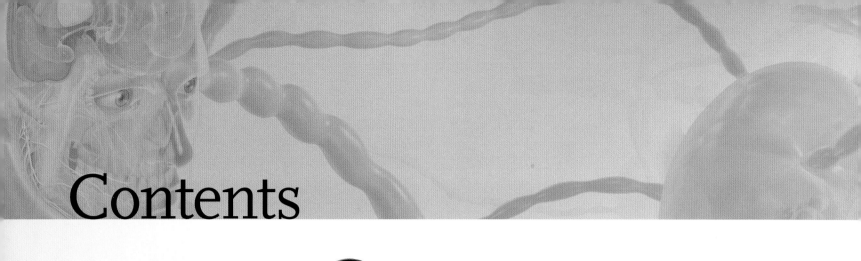

Contents

in *troducing*

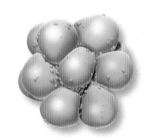
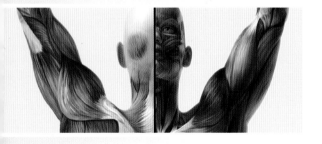

 *focus*

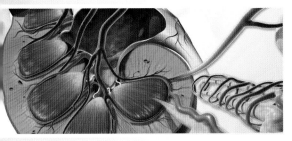

The Body's Systems

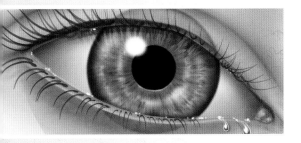

Senses

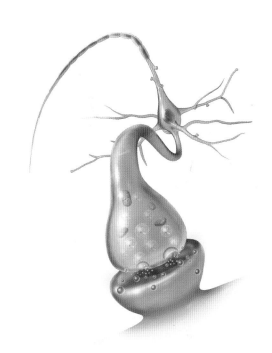

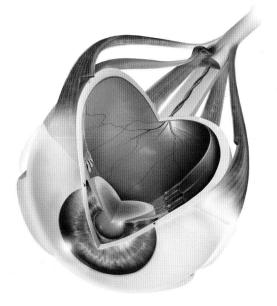

introducing

Cells

The Body's Building Blocks

The microscopic cell is the basic unit of life. All living organisms are made up of cells. Some organisms, such as bacteria, are just a single cell, but larger organisms, such as humans, consist of more than 10 trillion cells. There are about 200 different kinds of cells in the human body. Each is a highly organized unit and has a special job to do. Brain cells look different from blood cells, for example, and work in different ways. However, all the cells in the human body are needed and must cooperate so the body can function.

Divide and conquer
Mitosis occurs when a cell splits into two identical copies of itself. This process allows tissues to grow and heal.

Cytoplasm
This jelly-like substance holds all the parts of the cell in place.

Lysosome
These break down harmful or unwanted substances in the cell.

Nucleolus
All cell activity is controlled by this central area.

Nucleus
This is where chromosomes are stored.

Mitochondria
These cell parts make energy to fuel cell functions.

Centriole
Centrioles have an important role in mitosis.

A FAMILY OF CELLS

All cells have a similar basic structure, but they vary greatly in size, shape, and the functions they perform. The shape of the cell usually reflects the role it plays in the day-to-day working of the human body.

Y chromosome
The Y chromosome is found only in males. Males have one X and one Y chromosome.

X chromosome
The X chromosome is found in both males and females. Females have two X chromosomes.

Nerve cell
Nerve cells have only one long axon for outgoing signals and hundreds of shorter, branching dendrites to transmit incoming signals.

Axon

Dendrite

Smooth muscle cell
These elastic cells allow movement in tissues and organs, such as the intestines, that humans do not consciously control.

White blood cell
These cells form part of the body's defense against invading germs. Their outer layer helps attract, trap, and destroy germs.

Sperm cell The long tail of a male's sperm cell helps it swim through fluid to find and fertilize a female's egg.

Different, but the same . . .
Humans begin life as a single cell that multiplies. The new cells take on different roles and functions, but they all contain an identical copy of their genetic blueprint, known as DNA.

Cell membrane
The cell membrane controls the movement of substances into and out of the cell.

Body code *DNA, or deoxyribonucleic acid, is found in the cell's nucleus. It contains coded information for how all cells are made, behave, and function. DNA is unique to each person.*

Growth and Aging

A body grows most rapidly in the first two years of life. This is also a time of rapid mental development as skills such as walking and talking are learned and mastered. Physical growth continues through childhood to puberty, when a child matures into an adult. A person is usually fully physically grown around the age of 20. After this, new cells continue to be made, but they simply replace old cells rather than cause further growth. Over time, there is a gradual decrease in cell production, leading to signs of aging, such as wrinkling of the skin and gray hair.

All change *As children grow, they become more able to think for themselves and take responsibility. Young teenagers develop the physical signs of adulthood during puberty.*

Reflex action *At birth, babies weigh around 7.5 pounds (3.5 kg) and are about 18 inches (50 cm) in length. They have little coordination, and their movements are often simple reflexes, such as grasping.*

Growing stronger *Children grow not only in height and weight, but also in strength. Their ability to do tasks that require precise movements, such as writing and drawing, develops.*

THE EYES HAVE IT

3 years old

15 years old

30 years old

Production slows *The body's production of fewer cells is the major cause of the signs of aging. Fewer muscle cells reduce strength; fewer bone cells make bones weaker; and fewer brain cells may cause memory problems.*

No taller *Fully grown adults are 20 times bigger than newborns. Exercise and training can improve strength, endurance, and flexibility but will not change a person's height.*

Developmental milestones

As children grow, they usually develop different skills by particular ages—these are known as developmental milestones. Examples of these include sitting up by the age of six months, speaking their first words by the age of twelve months, and running by the age of two years.

50 years old

80 years old

Timeline of Medical Knowledge

ANCIENT MEDICINE

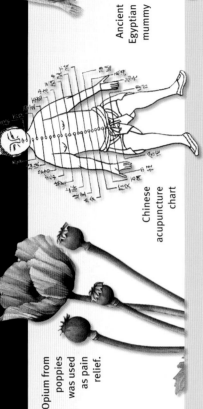

Cave painting of witch doctor

ANCIENT MEDICINE
Remains from 50,000 years ago show humans tried to set broken bones in natural positions. But medicine was more religion than science in ancient times.

Opium from poppies was used as pain relief.

Chinese acupuncture chart

Ancient Egyptian mummy

GREEK AND ROMAN

Asclepius —Greek god of medicine

Claudius Galen (AD 129–199) wrote extensively about the human body.

The four humors

Hippocrates—the father of Western medicine

GREEK AND ROMAN
Western medicine began when the Greeks and Romans looked beyond superstitions and searched for rational explanations about how the body worked and what caused illness.

ARABIC MEDICINE

Ottoman drawing of surgical techniques

Herbs, such as ginger, were valued medicines and were documented in Arabic manuscripts.

Al-Razi—Arabic medical scholar

ARABIC MEDICINE
The Arabic empire, with its increasing interest in medicine, made advances in general knowledge about illness. The Arabs also developed a systematic approach to prescribing drugs.

ARABIC MEDICINE

Trepanning (boring a hole in the skull)

Amulet to protect against the Great Plague (1346–47)

Leeches used for bloodletting

Astrology was considered a branch of medical practice.

MIDDLE AGES
Medicine in the Middle Ages was a combination of folk remedies, pagan superstition, and magic. Illness was still believed to be the result of an imbalance of key

MIDDLE AGES

RENAISSANCE

By the 1500s, artists and scientists were freeing themselves of religious traditions and began working directly with nature. The result was a greater understanding of the human body and how it works.

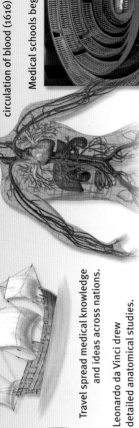

Travel spread medical knowledge and ideas across nations.

Leonardo da Vinci drew detailed anatomical studies.

William Harvey discovered the circulation of blood (1616).

Medical schools began teaching anatomy.

RENAISSANCE

18TH AND 19TH CENTURIES

Military surgery flourished throughout the 18th and 19th centuries, and with it came a greater understanding of anatomy and infection, as well as anesthesia.   Florence Nightingale

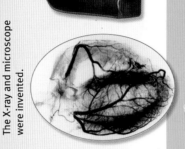

Chloroform was used for anesthesia.

The X-ray and microscope were invented.

Vaccinations were developed, including one for smallpox.

Germs were discovered as the cause of infection.

18TH AND 19TH CENTURIES

20TH CENTURY

In the 20th century, major discoveries were made, diseases were diagnosed, and new treatments and drugs were developed.
Life expectancy dramatically increased in developed countries.

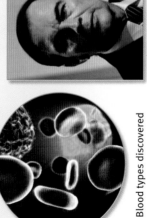

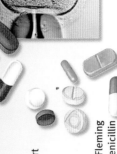

Blood types discovered

Christiaan Barnard performed the first heart transplant (1967).

Alexander Fleming discovered penicillin (1929).

The first baby was born through IVF (1978).

HIV/AIDS was first recognized (early 1980s).

20TH CENTURY

21ST CENTURY

While genetic treatments and therapeutic cloning dominate modern-day headlines, scientific research continues to seek answers for old diseases such as diabetes, heart disease, and cancer.

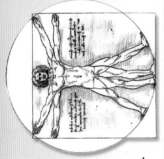

Mapping the genes in human DNA

Avian bird flu

Stem cell—medical miracle of the future?

Dolly—the first successfully cloned mammal (1997)

21ST CENTURY

Bionic Body

Technology has come to the aid of many people who, for reasons of disease or accident, need to have a body part replaced. Some parts, such as joints and teeth, are replaced with man-made materials. Other parts of the body need replacements from humans. Organs, such as hearts and corneas, are transplanted from people who have just died. Blood, bone marrow, and even a single kidney, can be received from living donors. Sometimes a person's own body can be used to supply replacement parts, as with skin grafts.

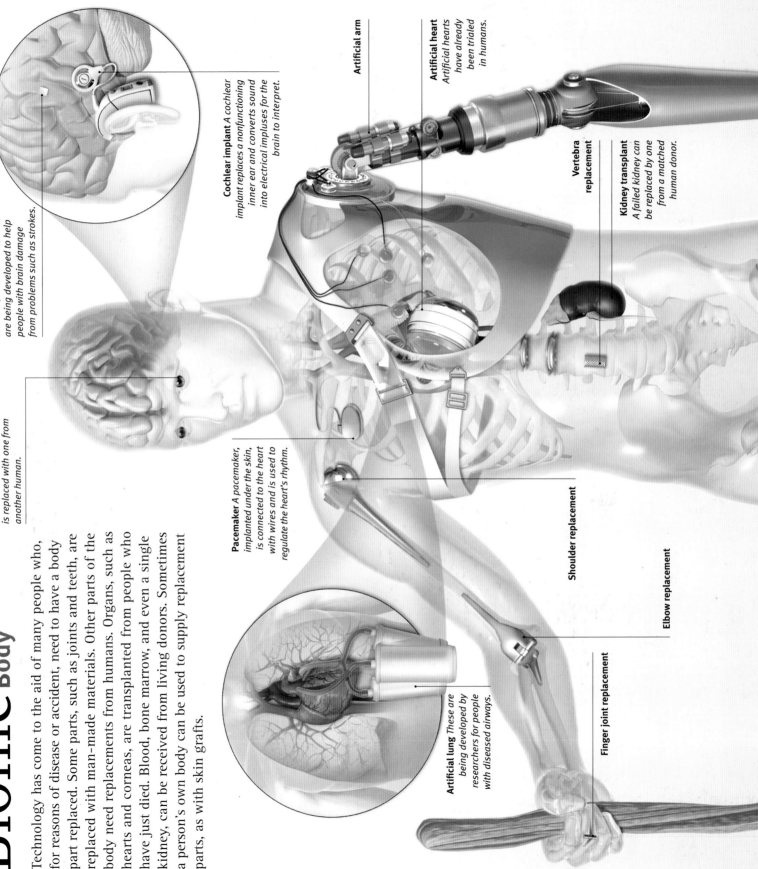

Brain implant *Brain implants are being developed to help people with brain damage from problems such as strokes.*

Cornea transplant *This is when a damaged cornea is replaced with one from another human.*

Cochlear implant *A cochlear implant replaces a nonfunctioning inner ear and converts sound into electrical impluses for the brain to interpret.*

Artificial arm

Artificial heart *Artificial hearts have already been trialed in humans.*

Vertebra replacement

Kidney transplant *A failed kidney can be replaced by one from a matched human donor.*

Pacemaker *A pacemaker, implanted under the skin, is connected to the heart with wires and is used to regulate the heart's rhythm.*

Shoulder replacement

Elbow replacement

Finger joint replacement

Artificial lung *These are being developed by researchers for people with diseased airways.*

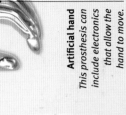

Artificial hand
This prosthesis can include electronics that allow the hand to move.

Bone marrow transplant
Transplanted bone marrow from a living donor provides a source of new, nondiseased cells.

Total knee replacement

Skin graft *A skin graft can come from a person's own body or can be synthetic.*

Ankle replacement

Toe joint replacement

Total hip replacement *A total hip replacement uses very strong, man-made materials to create a ball-and-socket joint.*

Walking stick *Despite advances in technology, some traditional aids, such as the simple stick, are still valuable in assisting human function, in this case walking.*

Artificial leg *An artificial leg has a hinged knee joint and can be given a realistic appearance.*

Keep on moving

Sometimes, rather than replacing faulty body parts with living tissue, man-made devices are used to replace that part's function. Examples include the cochlear implant that lets deaf people hear and the cardiac pacemaker that sends electrical impulses to the heart, ensuring the heartbeat remains regular.

From the
Inside Out

In early times, the human body and how it worked was largely a mystery, often explained by superstition and religious teachings. In Europe, it was not until the Renaissance in the 1500s that scientists began to question these beliefs. They started dissecting human corpses in an effort to understand the body and the diseases that affected it. In the late 1800s, with the invention of X-rays, doctors were able to see what was happening under the skin without having to cut open the patient. Since then, many other technologies have been developed, providing more and more valuable information about the inner workings of the human body.

Man *These MRI scans are made up of many separate scans of sections of the body, which are then combined.*

THE PILL CAMERA

Doctors can use a pill camera to see what is happening in a patient's digestive system. The patient swallows the pill, then digital images are relayed at intervals from the pill to an external recorder.

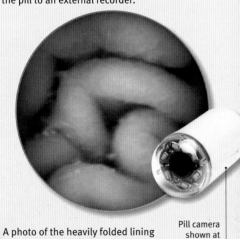

A photo of the heavily folded lining of the stomach, taken by a pill camera

Pill camera shown at actual size

Many ways

There are several types of scanning devices, each of which uses a different method to see inside. For example, computerized tomography (CT) uses X-ray beams, ultrasounds use sound waves, and magnetic resonance imaging (MRI) uses a strong magnetic field and radio waves.

Child *The dark oval seen in the pelvis is the bladder.*

Bones *The white areas of the scan are bones.*

Sharp shooting
The first time X-rays were used to help in surgery was in February 1896. Professor Michael Pupin of Columbia University x-rayed the hand of a man who had accidentally been shot with a shotgun.

Woman *The two black areas in the chest are the lungs.*

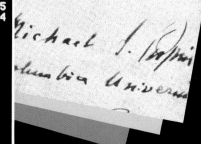

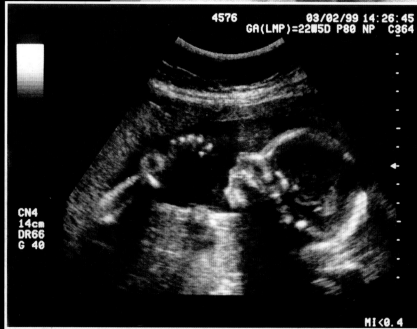

Sound advice
Ultrasound scanning was developed in the 1950s. High-pitched sound waves are directed into the body, and the echoes these sound waves create are recorded. Ultrasounds are used to check babies in the womb.

Skeleton

The skeleton is the bony inner scaffolding that gives the body shape. On average, an adult's skeleton contains 206 bones. A newborn baby actually has more than 300 bones, but as we grow, our bones grow longer and stronger, and some of them fuse together, reducing the total number. The bones of the skeleton come in many shapes and sizes, which often reflect their function. For instance, the longest and strongest bones are found in the legs, which have to carry almost the entire body weight when walking or running. Bones make up about a quarter of a person's total body weight.

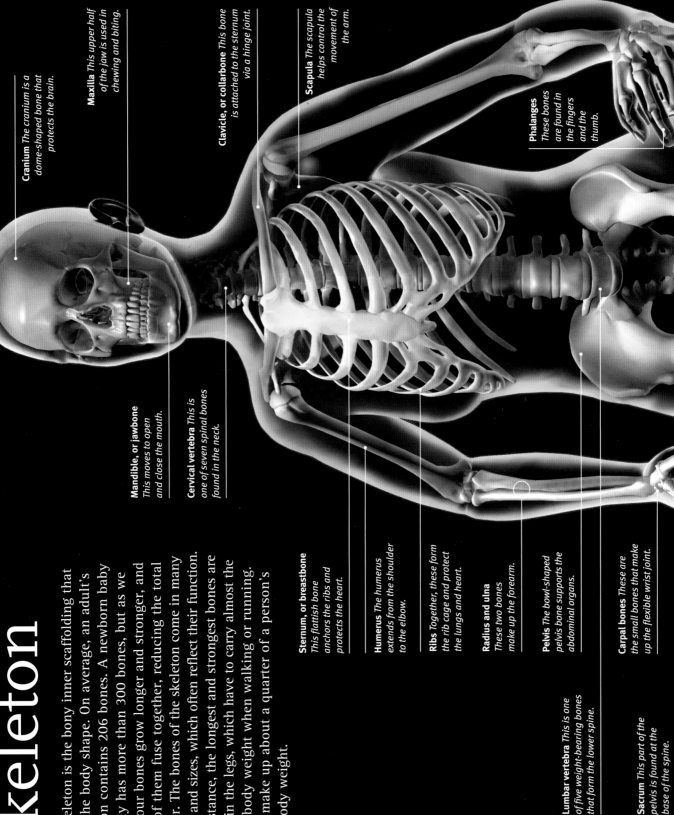

Cranium *The cranium is a dome-shaped bone that protects the brain.*

Maxilla *This upper half of the jaw is used in chewing and biting.*

Clavicle, or collarbone *This bone is attached to the sternum via a hinge joint.*

Scapula *The scapula helps control the movement of the arm.*

Phalanges *These bones are found in the fingers and the thumb.*

Head of femur *This bone connects with the pelvis at the ball-and-socket hip joint.*

Mandible, or jawbone *This moves to open and close the mouth.*

Cervical vertebra *This is one of seven spinal bones found in the neck.*

Sternum, or breastbone *This flattish bone anchors the ribs and protects the heart.*

Humerus *The humerus extends from the shoulder to the elbow.*

Ribs *Together, these form the rib cage and protect the lungs and heart.*

Radius and ulna *These two bones make up the forearm.*

Pelvis *The bowl-shaped pelvis bone supports the abdominal organs.*

Carpal bones *These are the small bones that make up the flexible wrist joint.*

Metacarpals *These five bones are found in the palm of the hand.*

Lumbar vertebra *This is one of five weight-bearing bones that form the lower spine.*

Sacrum *This part of the pelvis is found at the base of the spine.*

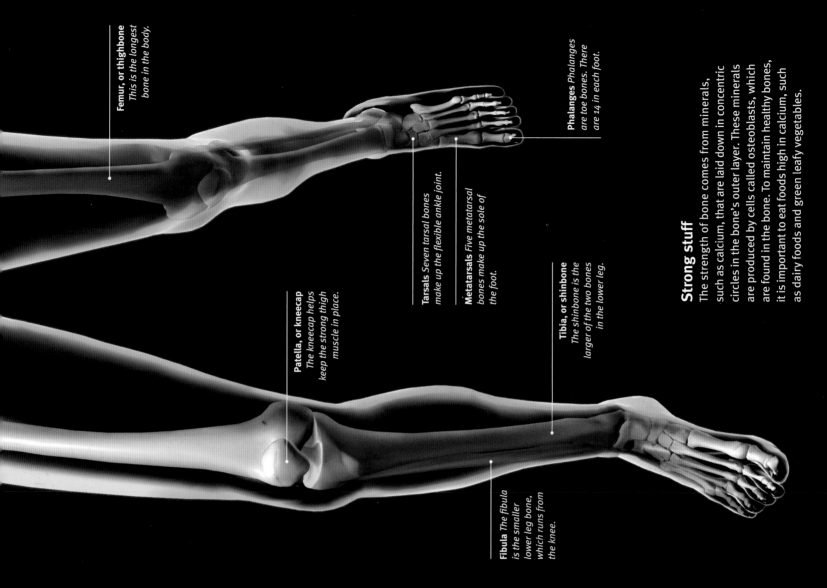

Femur, or thighbone *This is the longest bone in the body.*

Phalanges *Phalanges are toe bones. There are 14 in each foot.*

Tarsals *Seven tarsal bones make up the flexible ankle joint.*

Metatarsals *Five metatarsal bones make up the sole of the foot.*

Patella, or kneecap *The kneecap helps keep the strong thigh muscle in place.*

Tibia, or shinbone *The shinbone is the larger of the two bones in the lower leg.*

Fibula *The fibula is the smaller lower leg bone, which runs from the knee.*

Strong stuff

The strength of bone comes from minerals, such as calcium, that are laid down in concentric circles in the bone's outer layer. These minerals are produced by cells called osteoblasts, which are found in the bone. To maintain healthy bones, it is important to eat foods high in calcium, such as dairy foods and green leafy vegetables.

Adapted to give birth

The opening within a female's pelvis, known as the pelvic inlet, is much wider than a male's. The female's wider opening allows a baby to pass through during childbirth. The male pelvis is shown below as bone. The larger female pelvis is overlaid in pink.

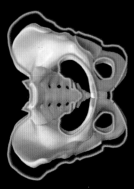

FROM THE BACK

The spine is made up of 24 vertebrae, which are separated by tough, rubbery disks that act like shock absorbers. These disks are made from cartilage; they make up 25 percent of the spine's length.

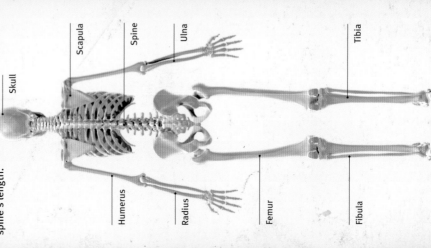

Skull

Scapula

Spine

Ulna

Humerus

Radius

Femur

Fibula

Tibia

At the Core
Bones

Although bones may appear hard, dry, and solid, they are actually living tissue containing blood vessels, nerves, and cells. We know them best as the framework for the human body, but they have many functions, including protecting internal organs and producing blood cells. Because bones are living tissue, new bone cells are continually being made to replace dying bone cells. This is why a fractured bone is able to heal. The strength of a bone comes from minerals, such as calcium, that are laid down in concentric circles in the bone's outer layer. These minerals are produced by cells called osteoblasts, found within the bone.

PROTECTION PLUS

Bone surfaces in joints are covered with shiny, slippery tissue called cartilage. Cartilage protects bones and helps joints move easily, such as the knee joint, which is used when sitting or walking.

Cartilage

Many uses Hyaline cartilage helps joints to move. But in other parts of the body, such as the nose, ear, and bronchi, its function is to give shape and strength.

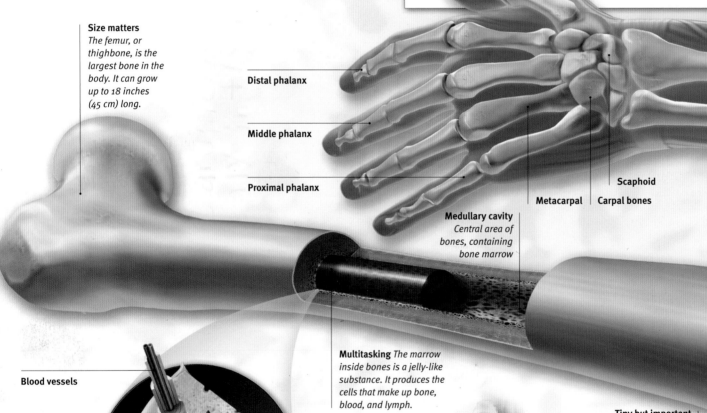

Size matters
The femur, or thighbone, is the largest bone in the body. It can grow up to 18 inches (45 cm) long.

Distal phalanx

Middle phalanx

Proximal phalanx

Scaphoid

Metacarpal **Carpal bones**

Medullary cavity
Central area of bones, containing bone marrow

Multitasking *The marrow inside bones is a jelly-like substance. It produces the cells that make up bone, blood, and lymph.*

Blood vessels

Good support
The hard, dense outer layer of bone is known as compact bone. It is strong enough to support the body.

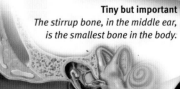

Tiny but important
The stirrup bone, in the middle ear, is the smallest bone in the body.

Call to arms

The shoulder, arm, and hand are incredibly flexible. They provide us with the ability to do a wide range of activities, from throwing a ball to writing or playing a musical instrument. This flexibility results from the coordination of the bones, joints, and muscles that make up our upper limb.

Scapula *Also known as the shoulder blade, this triangular bone in the back forms part of the shoulder joint.*

Humerus *The humerus is the* ___ *long bo___ upper___ the elbo___*

Radius *The radius is the shorter of the two bones that make up the forearm, connecting the elbow to the wrist.*

Ulna *The ulna is one of two long bones that make up the forearm.*

Lightweight *Spongy bone is the most elastic, lightweight bone tissue. It has a honeycomb appearance and lies under the hard outer layer of bone.*

JOINTS OF ALL KINDS

Joints are the places where two or more bones meet. Every bone in the human body joins with another bone, except for the hyoid bone in the neck. Joints have an important role to play and need to be strong enough to last through a lifetime of wear.

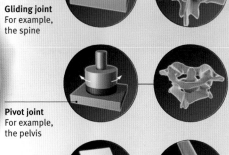

Gliding joint For example, the spine

Ball-and-socket joint For example, the shoulder

Pivot joint For example, the pelvis

Ellipsoid joint For example, the wrist

Hinge joint For example, the knee

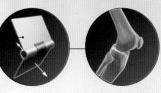

Saddle joint Found only in the thumb

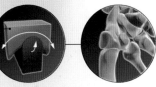

Muscles

The human body contains more than 600 muscles. There are three different types: skeletal muscle, smooth muscle, and cardiac muscle. Most muscles in the human body are skeletal muscles that we consciously control when we want to move. Smooth muscles work automatically and cause movement in internal organs such as the bladder. Cardiac muscle is found only in the heart, and its automatic movement is what causes the heart to beat.

Flexor carpi radialis *Forearm muscle that can flex the hand at the wrist or turn the hand outward.*

Brachioradialis *Muscle that flexes the elbow joint*

Biceps brachii *Bends the arm at the elbow, providing the opposite movement to the triceps brachii*

Sternocleidomastoid *Muscles in the neck that flex and rotate the head*

Pectoralis major *The main chest muscle, which helps pull the arm toward the body*

Heart wall *Cardiac muscle, found only in the wall of the heart, tirelessly contracts of its own accord at regular intervals.*

Rectus abdominis *Muscle at the front of the abdomen that helps us bend forward and sit up from lying down*

Interossei *Small muscles of the hands that produce a variety of finger movements*

Orbicularis oculi *Muscle surrounding the eye that helps close the lid*

Deltoid *Large shoulder muscle that allows the arm to be raised*

Triceps brachii *Allows the arm to straighten at the elbow*

Trapezius *Allows the shoulders to be shrugged and the head moved backward to look up*

Teres major *Attaches to the scapula and helps pull the arm toward the body*

Esophagus This smooth muscle in the wall of the throat allows food to be propelled from the mouth to the stomach.

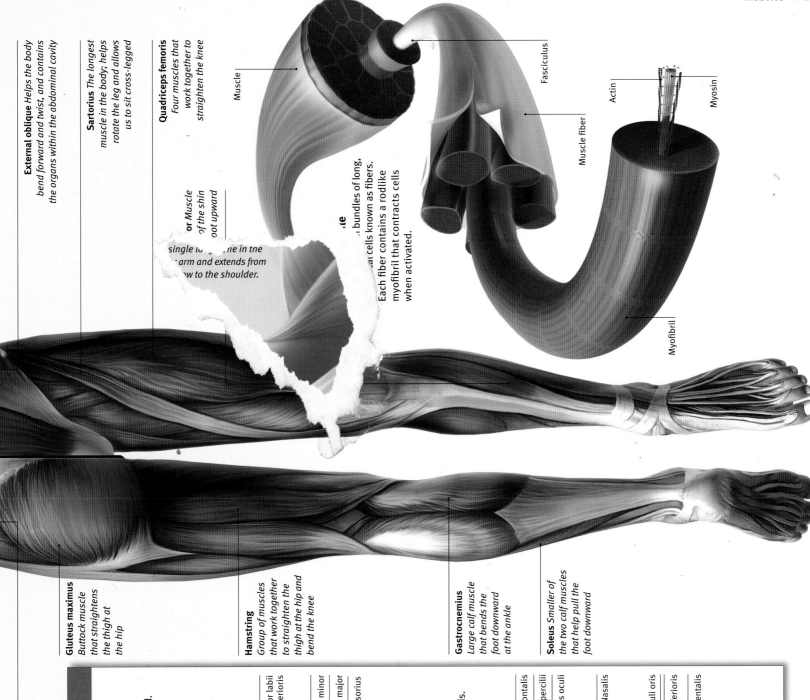

External oblique *Helps the body bend forward and twist, and contains the organs within the abdominal cavity*

Sartorius *The longest muscle in the body; helps rotate the leg and allows us to sit cross-legged*

Quadriceps femoris *Four muscles that work together to straighten the knee*

Muscle

Fasciculus

Muscle fiber

Actin

Myosin

Myofibril

...or Muscle *...of the shin ...oot upward*

...single ... ne in the ...arm and extends from ...ow to the shoulder.

...le

...bundles of long, ...at cells known as fibers. Each fiber contains a rodlike myofibril that contracts cells when activated.

Latissimus dorsi *Large, flat, triangular back muscle that helps with movement of the shoulder*

Gluteus maximus *Buttock muscle that straightens the thigh at the hip*

Hamstring *Group of muscles that work together to straighten the thigh at the hip and bend the knee*

Gastrocnemius *Large calf muscle that bends the foot downward at the ankle*

Soleus *Smaller of the two calf muscles that help pull the foot downward*

ALL IN THE FACE

The many facial expressions we are able to make are thanks to the contraction and relaxation of more than 50 facial muscles. Some of these muscles, known as levators, pull upward. Others, called depressors, pull downward.

Levator labii superioris

Zygomaticus minor

Zygomaticus major

Risorius

Smiling Smiling uses 12 major facial muscles to pull the lips upward, including the risorius, zygomaticus major, and the levator labii superioris.

Frontalis

Corrugator supercilii

Orbicularis oculi

Nasalis

Depressor anguli oris

Depressor labii inferioris

Mentalis

Frowning Contrary to popular myth, frowning uses fewer muscles than smiling—11 in fact, including the frontalis and the orbicularis oculi.

Skin, Hair, and Nails

...air, and nails make up the covering for the human body. Skin is the largest and heaviest organ. It covers almost 21.5 square feet (2 m²) ...ighs about 11 pounds (5 kg) in an adult. Not only does it act as a ...preventing water, germs, and dirt from entering the body, but skin ...important for sensation, temperature regulation, and fluid balance. ...re tough protectors that grow from the ends of fingers and toes. ...onstantly grow so that fingers and toes are always protected, even ...nails wear down through use. Hair also protects parts of the body ...e vulnerable to the environment. Like nails, it is made up of dead ...al, which explains why it does not hurt when it is cut. Both hair ...ils keep growing from the roots for the length of a human's life.

Skin deep In humans, skin varies in thickness, from 0.019 inches (0.5 mm) on the eyelids to up to 0.19 inches (5 mm) on the soles of the feet.

HARD AS NAILS

Nails are flat plates of keratin bonded together. They consist mostly of dead cells, except for the nail bed. Fingernails grow about two inches (5 cm) a year.

Cuticle

Body of nail

Proximal nail fold

Root of nail

Nail matrix

Bone of fingertip

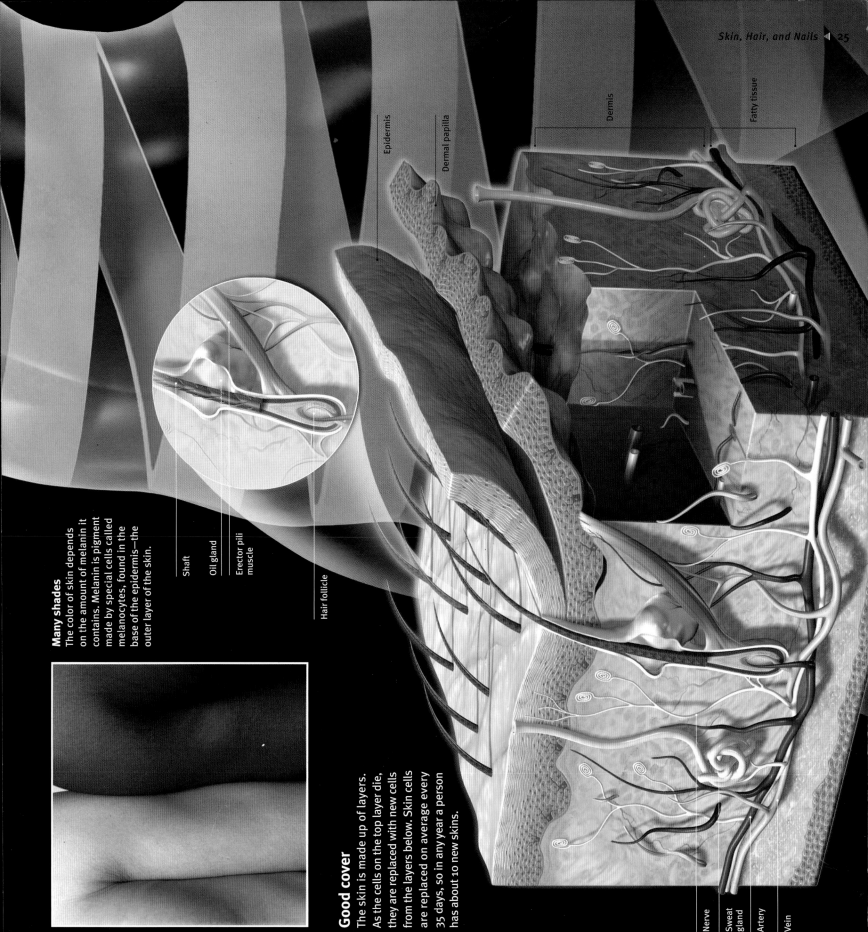

Epidermis

Dermal papilla

Dermis

Fatty tissue

Many shades

The color of skin depends on the amount of melanin it contains. Melanin is pigment made by special cells called melanocytes, found in the base of the epidermis—the outer layer of the skin.

Shaft

Oil gland

Erector pili muscle

Hair follicle

Good cover

The skin is made up of layers. As the cells on the top layer die, they are replaced with new cells from the layers below. Skin cells are replaced on average every 35 days, so in any year a person has about 10 new skins.

Nerve

Sweat gland

Artery

Vein

The Body in
Action

Exercise, such as running or swimming, makes muscles bigger and stronger. Muscles work by converting energy into power. They need a constant supply of fuel, including glycogen and oxygen. This is why when we exercise, our hearts beat faster, increasing the blood flow to our muscles. We also breathe harder to take in more oxygen. Healthy food and lots of exercise give muscles strength and staying power.

Men's 100 m sprint		
1912	Donald Lippincott	10.6 sec
1991	Carl Lewis	9.86 sec
2002	Tim Montgomery	9.78 sec

Women's 100 m hurdles		
1969	Teresa Sukniewicz	13.3 sec
1979	Graz˙yna Rabsztyn	12.48 sec
1988	Yordanka Donkova	12.21 sec

Faster, higher, farther
Why do people run faster, jump higher, and throw farther today than in the past? There are many possible reasons, from better nutrition to improved training and equipment. But scientists think that one day we will reach a limit as to how fast we can run or how high we can jump.

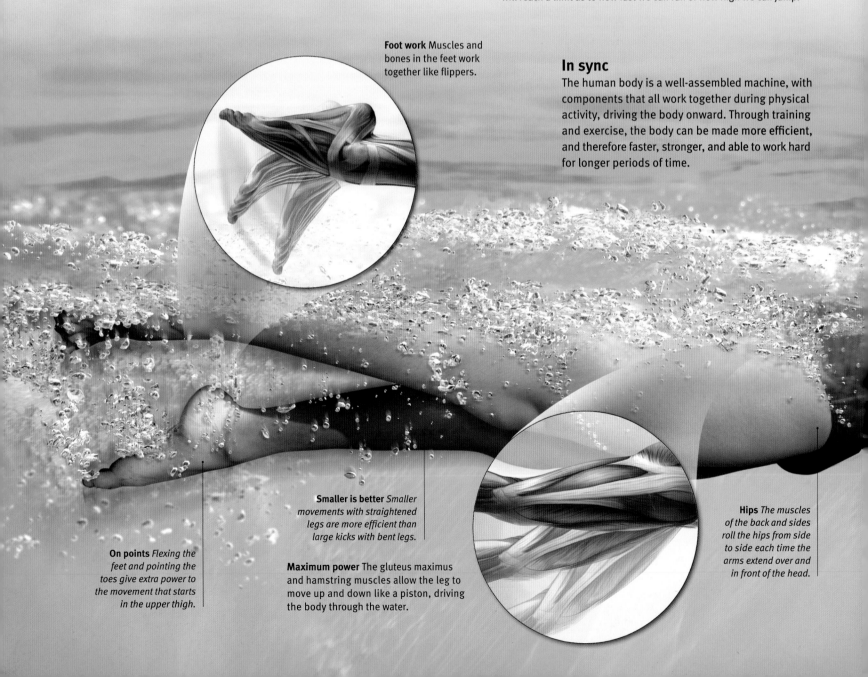

Foot work Muscles and bones in the feet work together like flippers.

In sync
The human body is a well-assembled machine, with components that all work together during physical activity, driving the body onward. Through training and exercise, the body can be made more efficient, and therefore faster, stronger, and able to work hard for longer periods of time.

On points *Flexing the feet and pointing the toes give extra power to the movement that starts in the upper thigh.*

Smaller is better *Smaller movements with straightened legs are more efficient than large kicks with bent legs.*

Maximum power The gluteus maximus and hamstring muscles allow the leg to move up and down like a piston, driving the body through the water.

Hips *The muscles of the back and sides roll the hips from side to side each time the arms extend over and in front of the head.*

Getting a good start

The swimmer gets into position on the starting block, crouched with his head down and leaning forward. At the starting signal, he pushes forward with his rear leg first and pushes his hands against the front of the block for extra momentum. As he leaves the starting block, he looks forward and flies through the air with his body stretched and streamlined. He stretches his arms toward the water and tucks his head down between his upper arms. To reduce resistance, he "pikes" at the waist to enter the water through the smallest possible area.

IMPORTANT: This dive should not be attempted in pools less than 6 feet (1.8 m) deep, due to the danger of neck injury.

Deep breath *To let the swimmer breathe, the head rolls from side to side in time with the body's rotation. The swimmer inhales as the arm extends, and exhales when the arm pulls back.*

Strength within The deltoid muscle in the shoulder and the triceps muscle in the upper arm give the arms mobility and pulling power.

Good support *The torso stays stretched and streamlined to support the spine and provide the least resistance to the water.*

Right around *The arms work like propellers. The upper arm muscles rotate around the shoulder joint as far as they can, then pull back.*

Paddle pressure *The hands act like paddles to trap water and lever the body through the water.*

In control Controlled breathing develops lung muscles and increases fitness. The lungs expand to take in more oxygen.

Organs

Organs are structures in the body that contain at least two different types of tissue, such as muscle and nerve tissue, and combine to perform a common function. There are many organs in the body, including the heart, the liver, and the skin. Often a number of organs will work together in what is called an organ system. A single organ system is usually responsible for performing one of the body's key functions. Examples of major organ systems include the skeletal system, the respiratory system, and the digestive system. None of these systems can work in isolation. They depend on one another to function properly.

Working together

Most organs are shaped to fit together in the confined space of the torso. If one stops working, the body cannot continue to function. Luckily, advances in science mean many organs can now be replaced or assisted.

Safe journey

Donor organs are transported in storage containers, which keep the organ cold and sterile. Donor kidneys can last for several days outside the body if stored correctly.

Brain *All the functions of the body are controlled by this organ.*

Skin *The body's largest organ, skin protects the body and maintains body temperature.*

Heart *The muscular heart pumps energy-giving blood to all parts of the body.*

Lung *Oxygen, needed by the body's cells, is absorbed in the lungs.*

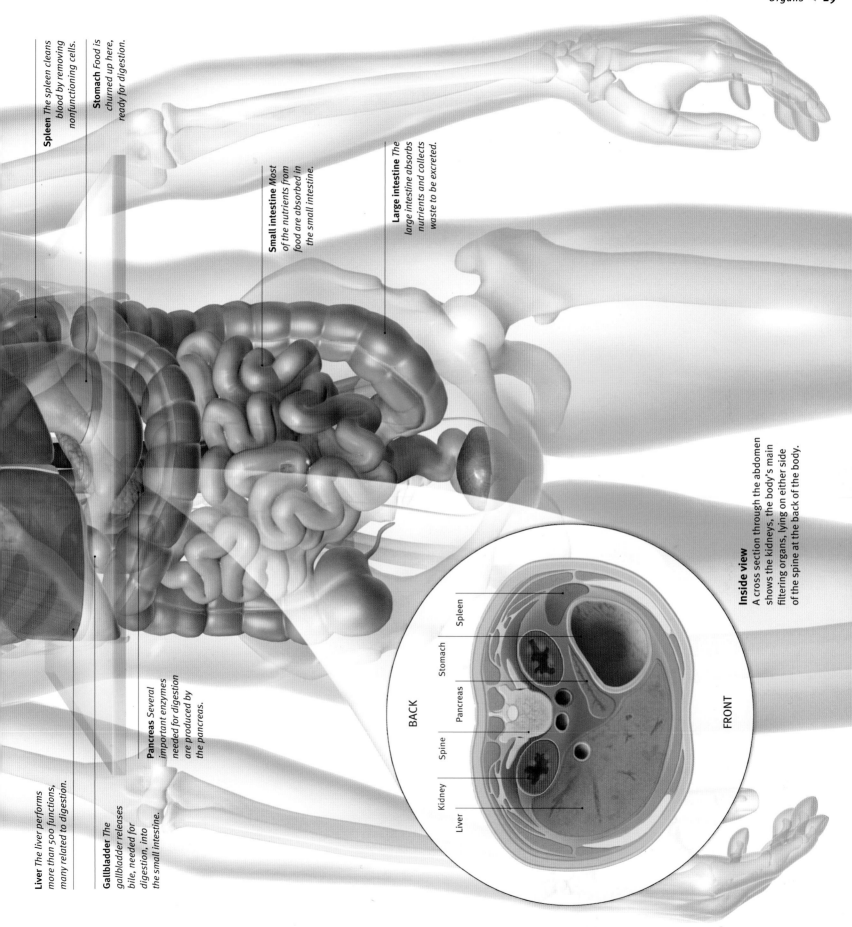

Spleen *The spleen cleans blood by removing nonfunctioning cells.*

Stomach *Food is churned up here, ready for digestion.*

Small intestine *Most of the nutrients from food are absorbed in the small intestine.*

Large intestine *The large intestine absorbs nutrients and collects waste to be excreted.*

Liver *The liver performs more than 500 functions, many related to digestion.*

Gallbladder *The gallbladder releases bile, needed for digestion, into the small intestine.*

Pancreas *Several important enzymes needed for digestion are produced by the pancreas.*

Inside view
A cross section through the abdomen shows the kidneys, the body's main filtering organs, lying on either side of the spine at the back of the body.

BACK

Spleen

Stomach

Pancreas

Spine

Kidney

Liver

FRONT

Life Force
Heart

The heart is a muscular pump that tirelessly pushes blood through the body, providing cells with oxygen and nutrients. Blood that has already delivered its oxygen is collected in the right receiving chamber of the heart, known as the right atrium. It then moves to the right ventricle, where it is pumped to the lungs through the pulmonary artery. In the lungs, the blood collects the oxygen needed by the body's cells. Once oxygenated, the blood returns from the lungs to the left atrium of the heart via the pulmonary vein. From there it is transferred to the left ventricle to be pumped to the rest of the body.

Broken hearted
The muscles of the heart have their own blood supply, known as coronary arteries. If a coronary artery becomes blocked, the muscle will not receive the blood it needs to function and will die. This is known as a heart attack.

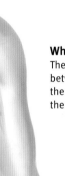

Where in the body
The heart lies in the chest, between the lungs and behind the sternum. It is tilted toward the left side of the body.

Right pulmonary artery
This artery carries oxygen-poor blood to the right lung.

Superior vena cava
This artery returns oxygen-poor blood to the heart.

Right atrium

Tricuspid valve *This one-way valve allows blood to flow from the right atrium to the right ventricle.*

Right ventricle

Inferior vena cava *This blood vessel returns oxygen-poor blood to the heart.*

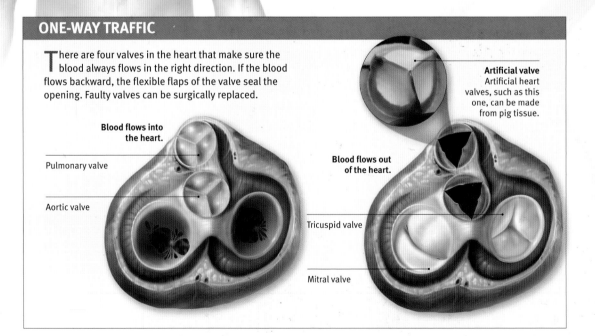

ONE-WAY TRAFFIC

There are four valves in the heart that make sure the blood always flows in the right direction. If the blood flows backward, the flexible flaps of the valve seal the opening. Faulty valves can be surgically replaced.

Blood flows into the heart.

Pulmonary valve

Aortic valve

Artificial valve
Artificial heart valves, such as this one, can be made from pig tissue.

Blood flows out of the heart.

Tricuspid valve

Mitral valve

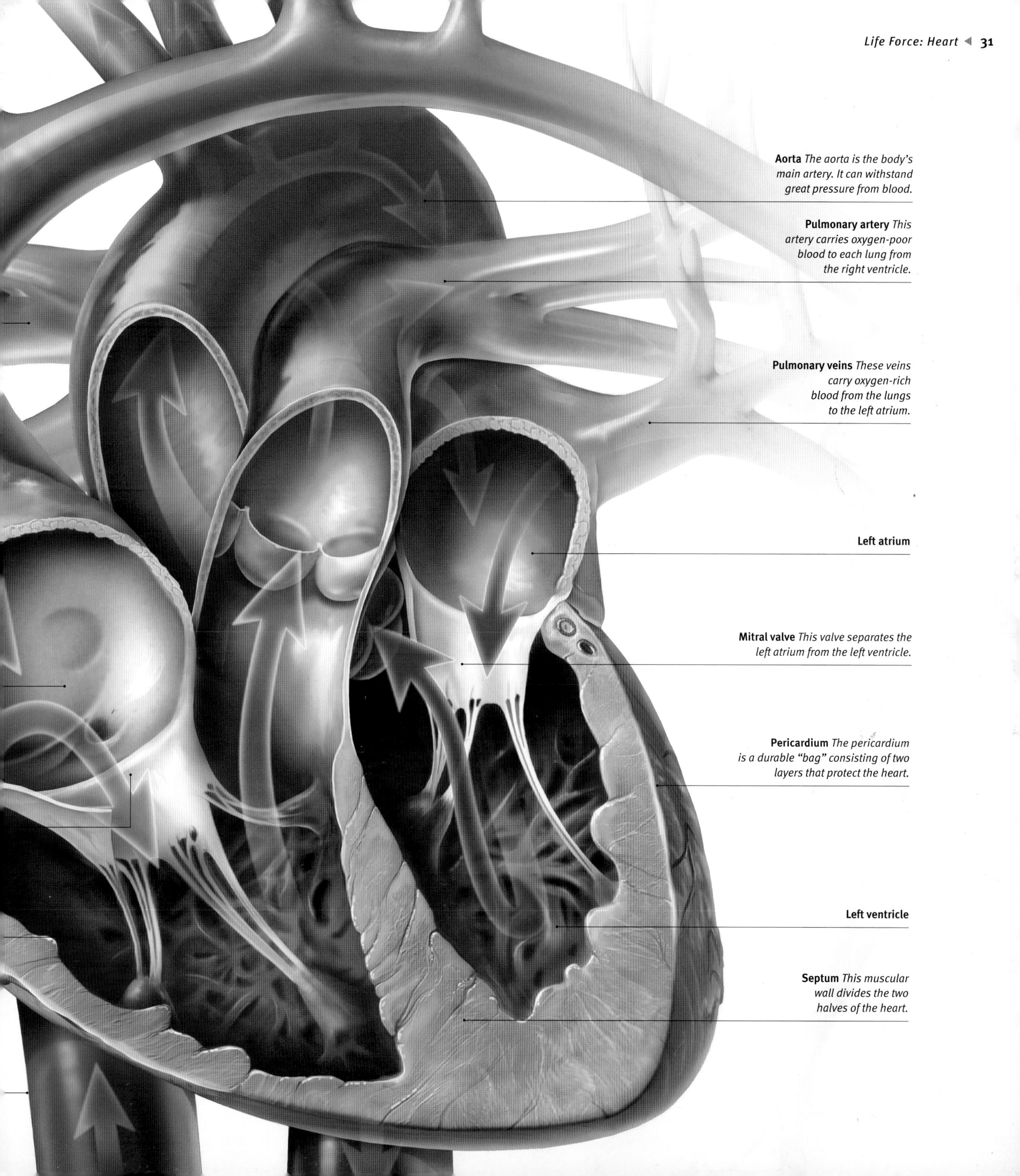

Aorta *The aorta is the body's main artery. It can withstand great pressure from blood.*

Pulmonary artery *This artery carries oxygen-poor blood to each lung from the right ventricle.*

Pulmonary veins *These veins carry oxygen-rich blood from the lungs to the left atrium.*

Left atrium

Mitral valve *This valve separates the left atrium from the left ventricle.*

Pericardium *The pericardium is a durable "bag" consisting of two layers that protect the heart.*

Left ventricle

Septum *This muscular wall divides the two halves of the heart.*

In Control
Brain

The brain is the control center of the entire body. It processes the information from incoming nerve signals so that a person knows what he or she sees, smells, and tastes, as well as whether he or she is hot, hungry, or in pain. The brain also generates outgoing nerve signals to control the body's activities, from walking to sweating. Memory, feelings, and imagination are all functions of the billions of brain cells.

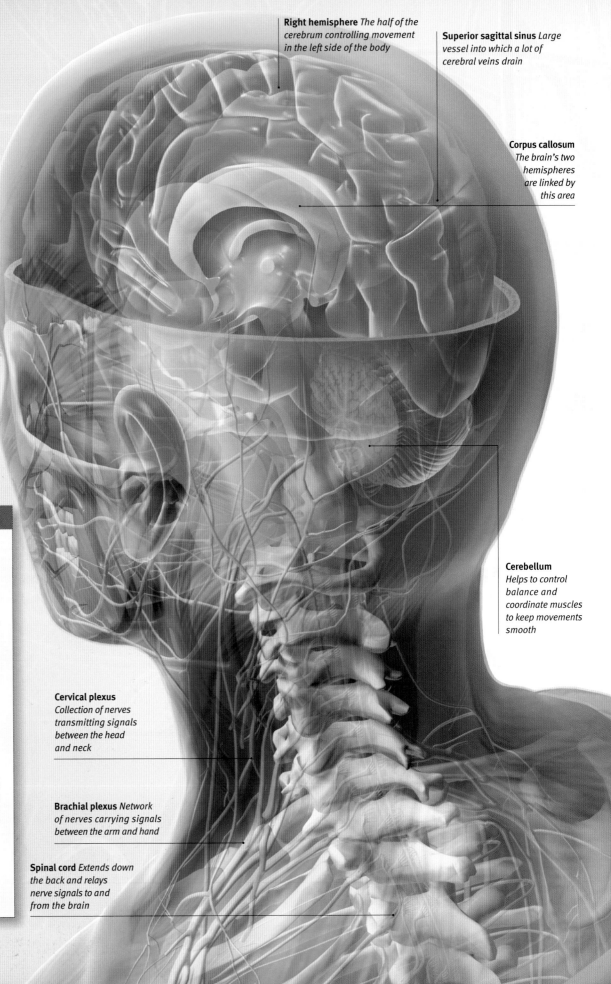

Right hemisphere *The half of the cerebrum controlling movement in the left side of the body*

Superior sagittal sinus *Large vessel into which a lot of cerebral veins drain*

Corpus callosum *The brain's two hemispheres are linked by this area*

Cerebellum *Helps to control balance and coordinate muscles to keep movements smooth*

Cervical plexus *Collection of nerves transmitting signals between the head and neck*

Brachial plexus *Network of nerves carrying signals between the arm and hand*

Spinal cord *Extends down the back and relays nerve signals to and from the brain*

BRAIN WAVES

Separate areas of the cerebral cortex are used to enable a person to listen and speak. Brain scans allow us to see the areas used during different activities.

 Areas of the temporal lobe interpret the meanings of sounds as words.

 Monitoring speech uses a large area of the auditory cortex.

 Sounds are first detected by the auditory center in the temporal lobe.

 Areas called Wernicke's and Broca's regions are used to comprehend and generate speech.

Working as one

The brain is made up of three parts—the cerebrum, the cerebellum, and the brain stem. Each of the two halves of the cerebrum controls movement in the opposite side of the body. The cerebellum coordinates the movement, and the brain stem controls involuntary actions, such as breathing.

Cingulate gyrus
Area above the corpus callosum where most emotion is generated

Hippocampus
Area involved with emotion, and where memories are formed

Amygdala
Deals with emotion, memory, and fear

Thalamus
Acts as the "sorting center" by directing signals into and out of the brain

Pituitary gland
Produces hormones that control body functions such as growth

Pons *Part of the brain stem involved in motor control and interpreting sensory signals*

Medulla oblongata
Looks after involuntary body functions such as breathing

Brain stem

Facial nerve
Controls the movement of many of the major muscles of the face

SIGHT

SMELL

TASTE

HEARING

TOUCH

Senses bar The colored bar provides you with easy reference to the sense being discussed on the spread.

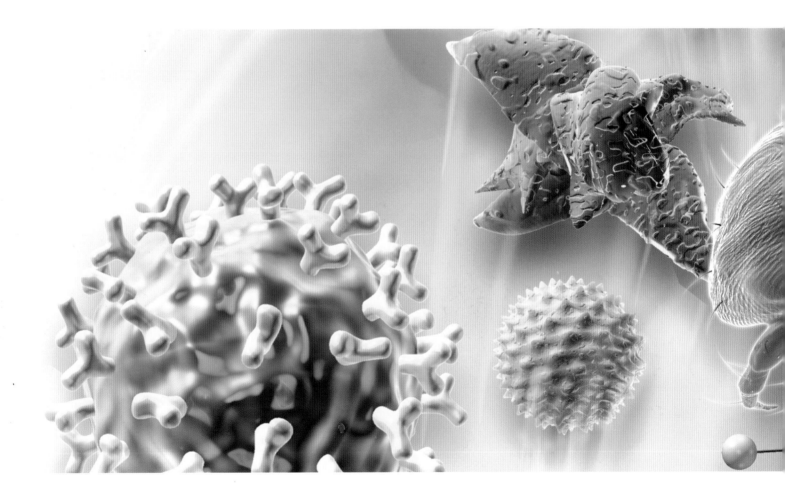

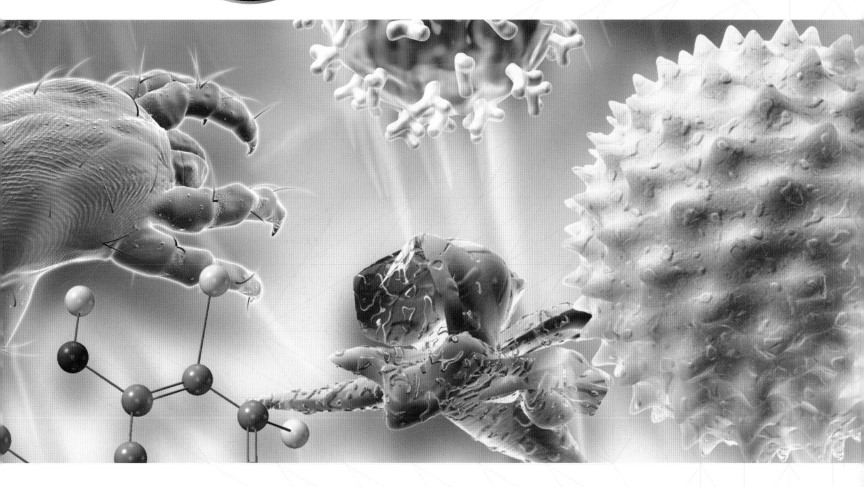

Respiration

Breathing is so natural that most of the time we are unaware we are doing it, yet it is vital to keeping the body alive. The purpose of breathing is to absorb oxygen (O_2) into the bloodstream and to expel the waste product, carbon dioxide (CO_2), out of the body. This process is called respiration. Oxygen is used by most cells in the body, but the human body is unable to store much oxygen, so it has to keep breathing. The body needs more than a gallon (5 l) of air a minute, meaning a human has to take about 20,000 breaths a day. The brain regulates the rate of breathing depending on the levels of oxygen and carbon dioxide in the bloodstream.

Breath of life

With every breath, more than 15 ounces (500 ml) of air is taken into the lungs. This air is transported through a branching network of hollow tubes until it reaches the tiny air sacs known as alveoli, where oxygen is absorbed and carbon dioxide is expelled.

SHORT ON AIR

Asthma is a disease that results in shortness of breath and wheezing. It is often triggered by allergens that cause the lining of the airways to swell.

Dust mites are a common trigger of asthma attacks.

Allergies to pollen can also cause asthma.

A puffer or inhaler delivers medication directly to the swollen airways.

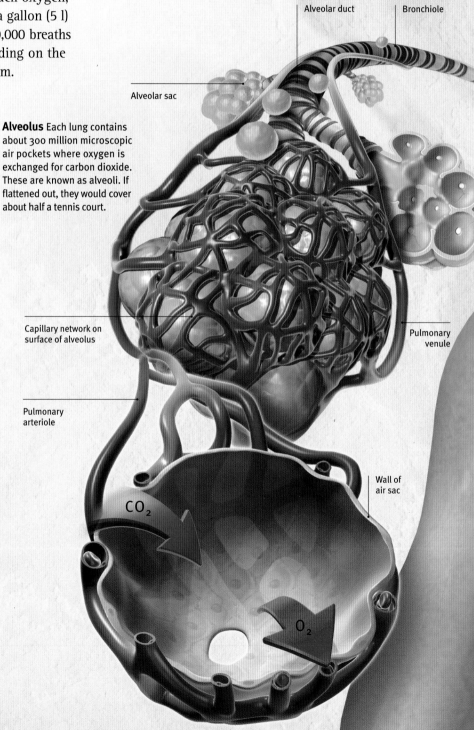

Alveolar duct

Bronchiole

Alveolar sac

Alveolus Each lung contains about 300 million microscopic air pockets where oxygen is exchanged for carbon dioxide. These are known as alveoli. If flattened out, they would cover about half a tennis court.

Capillary network on surface of alveolus

Pulmonary venule

Pulmonary arteriole

Wall of air sac

CO_2

O_2

Nose *The nose transports air to the throat. It is lined with sticky mucus and fine hairs that trap dirt and germs.*

INHALED GAS CONCENTRATIONS

Other gases

EXHALED GAS CONCENTRATIONS

Other gases

Carbon dioxide

Carbon dioxide

Oxygen

Oxygen

It's a gas Inhaled air contains about 20 percent oxygen and less than 1 percent carbon dioxide. The rest is mostly nitrogen. Exhaled air contains about 4 percent carbon dioxide and 15 percent oxygen.

Mouth

Larynx *The larynx, or voice box, is located at the top of the trachea. It contains the vocal cords.*

Pharynx *This contains the epiglottis, a flap that prevents food from going into the lungs when swallowing.*

Bronchi *These are the large, air-carrying tubes that branch off the trachea.*

Trachea *The trachea, or windpipe, runs from the larynx into the chest.*

Bronchiole *The smallest air passage of the bronchial tree, each bronchiole ends in a cluster of alveoli.*

Lung

Diaphragm *This curved muscle contracts to draw air into the lungs and also divides the chest cavity from the abdominal contents.*

Circulation

The circulatory, or cardiovascular, system transports blood to every single cell in the body. This blood supplies vital nutrients and oxygen to the body's tissues, as well as collecting and removing waste. It also carries cells to fight infection and helps control body temperature. The system is powered by a muscular pump—the heart. The blood leaves the heart in large, stretchy vessels known as arteries. Once the nutrients and oxygen have been delivered to the tissues, the blood returns to the heart in thinner-walled vessels known as veins. This circuit is completed up to three times every minute.

Carotid artery
This artery is the chief supplier of blood to the head and the brain.

Superior vena cava
This returns blood to the carotid artery to be reoxygenated.

Aorta *Oxygen-rich blood leaves the heart through the aorta, which is the largest blood vessel in the body.*

Atrium

Pulmonary vessels
The pulmonary artery takes oxygen-poor blood from the lungs. Once oxygenated, the blood returns to the heart via the pulmonary vein.

Heart *The heart is the body's pump and is made up of cardiac muscle—a unique muscle that never stops moving.*

Inferior vena cava
This is one of the main veins that carry blood back to the heart.

Renal artery and vein
These carry blood to and from the kidneys.

Networking

Blood travels around the body through a system of arteries, capillaries, and veins. Within the body there are about 60,000 miles (100,000 km) of blood vessels. Placed end to end, the blood vessels in the human body would stretch around the world twice.

Iliac artery *This artery branches off the aorta to supply blood to the pelvis and lower limbs.*

Femoral artery
This supplies the thigh and the lower leg with blood.

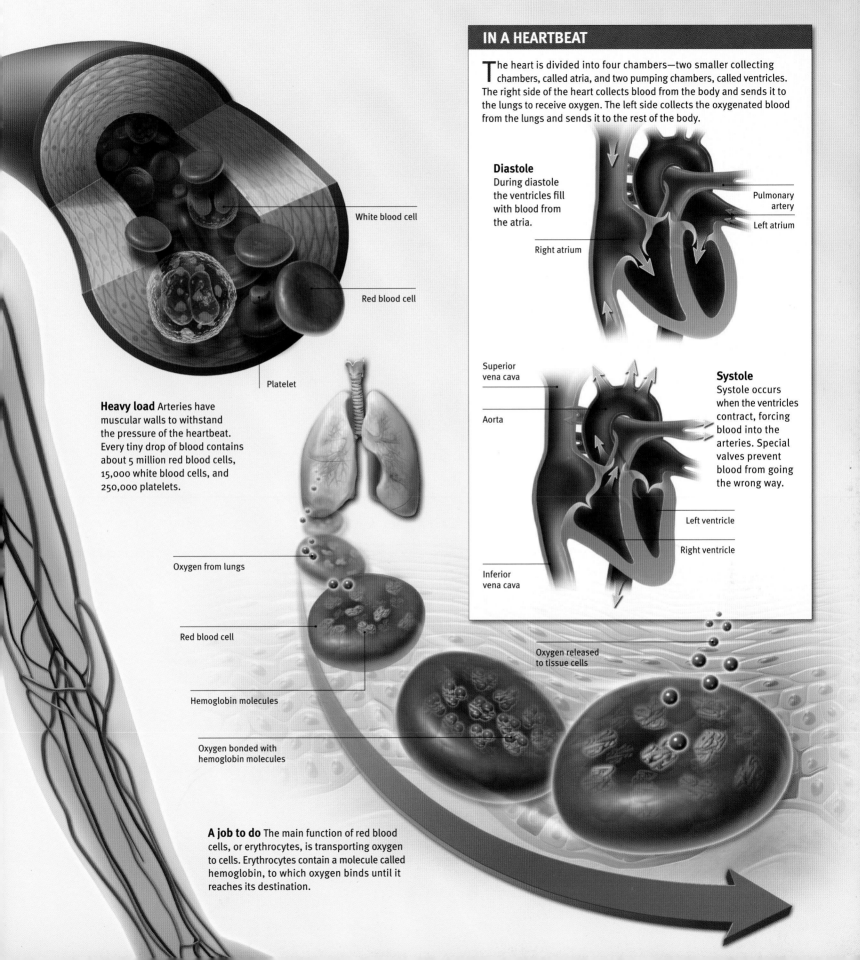

White blood cell

Red blood cell

Platelet

Heavy load Arteries have muscular walls to withstand the pressure of the heartbeat. Every tiny drop of blood contains about 5 million red blood cells, 15,000 white blood cells, and 250,000 platelets.

Oxygen from lungs

Red blood cell

Hemoglobin molecules

Oxygen bonded with hemoglobin molecules

A job to do The main function of red blood cells, or erythrocytes, is transporting oxygen to cells. Erythrocytes contain a molecule called hemoglobin, to which oxygen binds until it reaches its destination.

Oxygen released to tissue cells

IN A HEARTBEAT

The heart is divided into four chambers—two smaller collecting chambers, called atria, and two pumping chambers, called ventricles. The right side of the heart collects blood from the body and sends it to the lungs to receive oxygen. The left side collects the oxygenated blood from the lungs and sends it to the rest of the body.

Diastole
During diastole the ventricles fill with blood from the atria.

Pulmonary artery

Left atrium

Right atrium

Superior vena cava

Aorta

Systole
Systole occurs when the ventricles contract, forcing blood into the arteries. Special valves prevent blood from going the wrong way.

Left ventricle

Right ventricle

Inferior vena cava

Nervous System

Every thought, sensation, and action that the body makes is controlled by the nervous system. This system includes the brain, the spinal cord, and the nerves. The system is comprised of trillions of interlinked cells known as neurons. Neurons are able to transmit information in the form of electrical impulses at very high speeds down their long, wirelike fibers. The electrical impulses travel from one neuron to another through junctions known as synapses. The spinal cord is a collection of nerve fibers sending messages to and from the brain. It is about 17.5 inches (45 cm) long and runs the length of the spine.

Brain The brain is the control center for the entire body.

Eyes These organs collect visual signals and transmit them to the brain.

Cerebellum This area of the brain coordinates balance and movement.

Brachial plexus The brachial plexus is a collection of nerves that controls the arm muscles.

Spinal cord This superhighway of nerves connects the brain with the rest of the body.

Radial nerve The muscles in the forearm are controlled by this nerve.

Subcostal nerve The abdominal muscles are controlled by this nerve.

Lumbar plexus This group of four linked spinal nerves supplies the leg muscles.

Sacral plexus This collection of nerves runs from the base of the spinal cord.

Femoral nerve The femoral nerve controls the muscles in the front of the thigh.

Pudendal nerve This is found in the pelvis and carries sensation from the anal area.

Intercostal nerves These control the muscles of the chest wall.

Iliohypogastric nerve This nerve transmits signals to the muscles of the buttocks and abdomen.

Median nerve This nerve runs through the wrist and controls the small muscles of the hand.

Genitofemoral nerve This nerve controls muscles in the groin and upper leg.

Ulnar nerve This nerve runs past the elbow to the little finger.

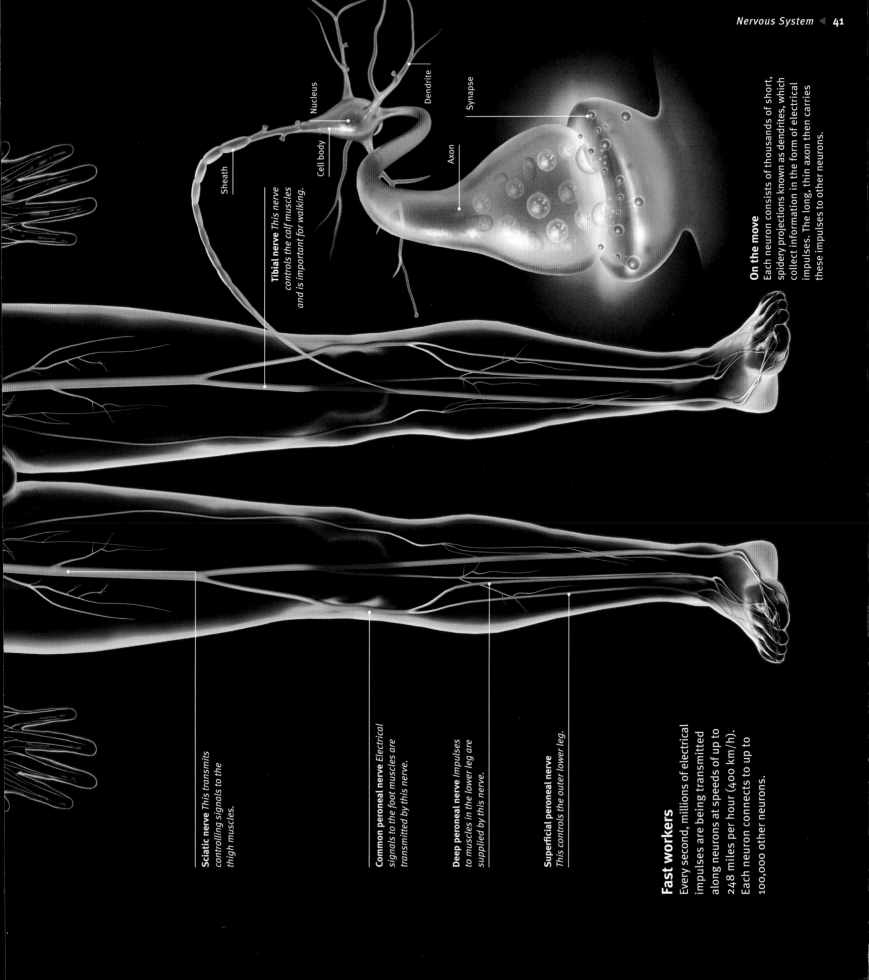

Dendrite

Synapse

Nucleus

Cell body

Axon

Sheath

Tibial nerve *This nerve controls the calf muscles and is important for walking.*

On the move
Each neuron consists of thousands of short, spidery projections known as dendrites, which collect information in the form of electrical impulses. The long, thin axon then carries these impulses to other neurons.

Sciatic nerve *This transmits controlling signals to the thigh muscles.*

Common peroneal nerve *Electrical signals to the foot muscles are transmitted by this nerve.*

Deep peroneal nerve *Impulses to muscles in the lower leg are supplied by this nerve.*

Superficial peroneal nerve *This controls the outer lower leg.*

Fast workers

Every second, millions of electrical impulses are being transmitted along neurons at speeds of up to 248 miles per hour (400 km/h). Each neuron connects to up to 100,000 other neurons.

The Body's
Defenses

The immune system is the body's defense against the disease-causing germs that are continually trying to invade it. The body has natural barriers, such as the skin and hair, but if a germ succeeds in getting past these barriers and enters the bloodstream, it is likely to encounter the body's killer white blood cells. There are five kinds of white blood cells, all of which have a role in defending against germ invaders. Some types, such as macrophages, consume and destroy the germ. A single macrophage can "eat" more than one hundred germs. Other cells, such as lymphocytes, create substances known as antibodies, which deactivate the germ, marking it for destruction.

TO THE RESCUE

When the body's first defense, skin, is breached, the immune system swiftly responds.

Help at hand When disease-carrying germs enter the bloodstream, the area becomes red and inflamed as the body mounts a defense.

To the rescue Blood vessels rush white blood cells to the injury site, where they trap and destroy invading germs and clear away dead cells.

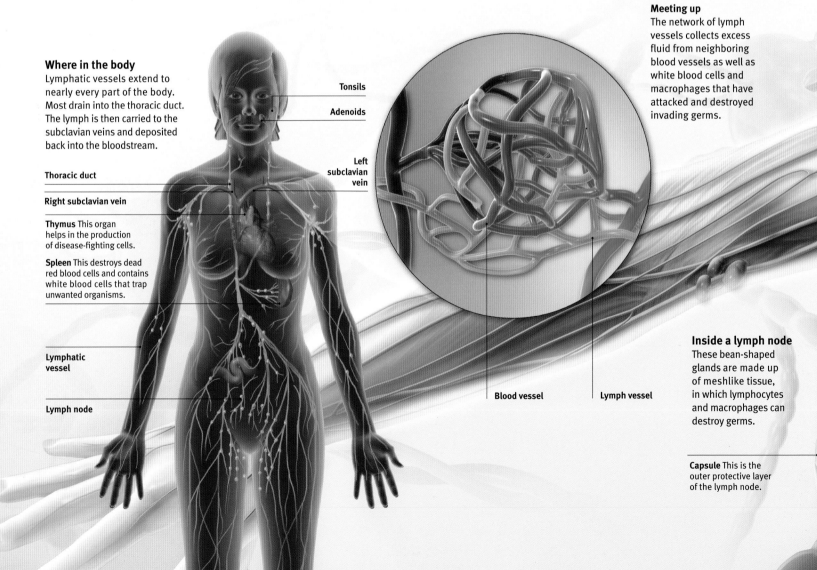

Where in the body
Lymphatic vessels extend to nearly every part of the body. Most drain into the thoracic duct. The lymph is then carried to the subclavian veins and deposited back into the bloodstream.

Thoracic duct

Right subclavian vein

Thymus This organ helps in the production of disease-fighting cells.

Spleen This destroys dead red blood cells and contains white blood cells that trap unwanted organisms.

Lymphatic vessel

Lymph node

Tonsils

Adenoids

Left subclavian vein

Meeting up
The network of lymph vessels collects excess fluid from neighboring blood vessels as well as white blood cells and macrophages that have attacked and destroyed invading germs.

Blood vessel

Lymph vessel

Inside a lymph node
These bean-shaped glands are made up of meshlike tissue, in which lymphocytes and macrophages can destroy germs.

Capsule This is the outer protective layer of the lymph node.

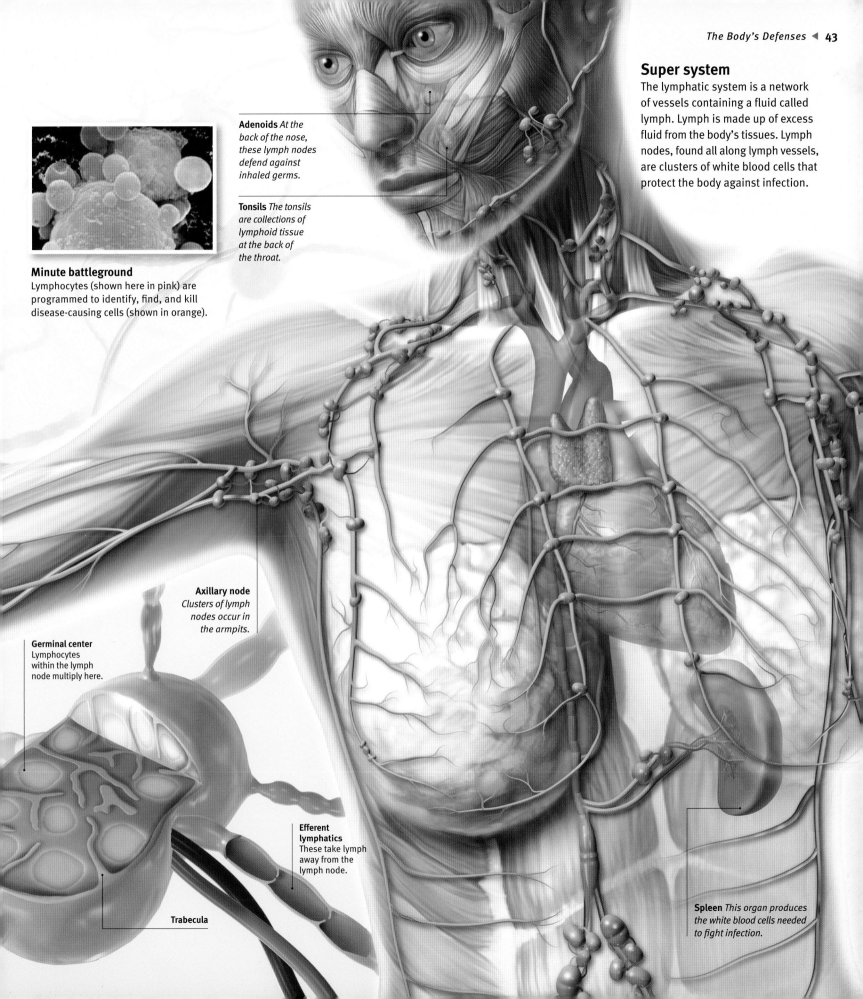

Adenoids *At the back of the nose, these lymph nodes defend against inhaled germs.*

Tonsils *The tonsils are collections of lymphoid tissue at the back of the throat.*

Super system

The lymphatic system is a network of vessels containing a fluid called lymph. Lymph is made up of excess fluid from the body's tissues. Lymph nodes, found all along lymph vessels, are clusters of white blood cells that protect the body against infection.

Minute battleground
Lymphocytes (shown here in pink) are programmed to identify, find, and kill disease-causing cells (shown in orange).

Axillary node *Clusters of lymph nodes occur in the armpits.*

Germinal center
Lymphocytes within the lymph node multiply here.

Efferent lymphatics
These take lymph away from the lymph node.

Trabecula

Spleen *This organ produces the white blood cells needed to fight infection.*

Digestive System

Long journey

The digestive tract is a 29.5-foot (9-m) muscular tube that runs from the mouth to the anus. Although we do not usually notice our bodies digesting the food we eat, the whole complex process, from chewing food to going to the bathroom, can take several days.

The body needs food to provide energy for growth, to fuel its many functions, and to renew its cells. In the digestive system, small chewed pieces of food first arrive at the stomach, where they are attacked by acids and powerful muscular contractions, which churn them into a creamy liquid. This liquid then enters the small intestine. Here, chemicals and digestive enzymes are added to the mix to aid the absorption of nutrients from food. In the large intestine, any residual nutrients, minerals, and water are absorbed from the intestine contents leaving undigested waste, which forms feces: the final product of the digestive process.

Mouth: 1 minute
Food is broken into smaller pieces and mixed with saliva.

Esophagus: 2–3 seconds
Food passes through here on its way to the stomach.

Stomach: 2–4 hours
Muscular movements and strong acids turn food into a paste.

Taste buds *These detect and send messages to the brain about the flavor of the food.*

Stomach wall *The folds in the stomach wall allow it to expand to up to 20 times its original size.*

Mouth *Food is crushed by teeth and mixed with saliva.*

Esophagus *The muscular wall of the esophagus propels chewed food from the mouth to the stomach.*

Liver *The liver processes and stores absorbed nutrients, and produces bile.*

Small intestine: 3–5 hours
Most minerals and liquids are absorbed from food here.

Large intestine: 10 hours–several days
Remaining minerals and liquids are absorbed here.

Ileum The ileum is the last part of the small intestine.

Large intestine Stretching around the borders of the abdomen is the large intestine.

Rectum The rectum is a muscular chamber for storing feces.

Anus The anus is the final stage of the digestive tract.

Sigmoid colon Any remaining water is absorbed in the sigmoid colon.

Villi The millions of 0.04-inch (1-mm)-long, finger-shaped villi increase the surface area of the small intestine.

Appendix No one knows what function the appendix has in humans.

Gallbladder The gallbladder stores and concentrates bile, needed to absorb fat.

Duodenum The duodenum is the first part of the small intestine.

Stomach The stomach contains acids corrosive enough to strip paint.

Jejunum This central part of the small intestine is full of intestinal villi.

Cecum The cecum is the first part of the large intestine beyond the appendix.

MEASURING UP

The small intestine is about 20 feet (6 m) long, which is four times the length of the large intestine. However, the large intestine got its name because it is much wider than the small intestine.

Small intestine The small intestine, measuring about 1 inch (2.5 cm) in diameter, is where most nutrients are absorbed.

Large intestine The large intestine, measuring 5.5 inches (14 cm) in diameter, absorbs water and minerals from food.

Urinary System

Filtering the blood and getting rid of waste products are the main functions of the body's urinary system, and in particular, the kidneys. The two kidneys constantly cleanse blood, at a rate of about 450 gallons (1,700 l) a day. The cleansed blood is then returned to the circulatory system and distributed around the body. The kidneys contain nephrons, thousands of tiny filtering units, used to filter out harmful waste and excess water. This process produces urine. Urine drains down waterproof tubes, known as ureters, and into the bladder, where it is stored until it is released from the body through the urethra.

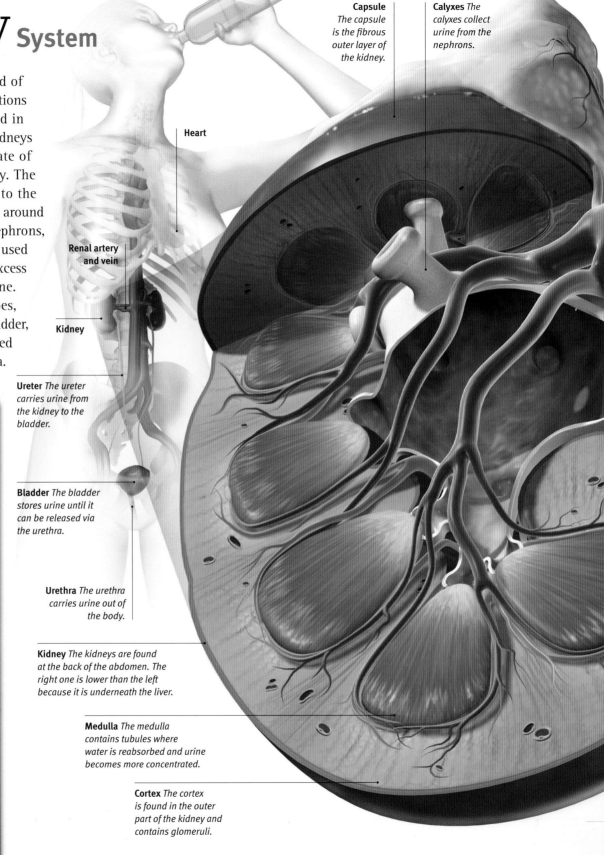

Heart

Renal artery and vein

Kidney

Capsule *The capsule is the fibrous outer layer of the kidney.*

Calyxes *The calyxes collect urine from the nephrons.*

Ureter *The ureter carries urine from the kidney to the bladder.*

Bladder *The bladder stores urine until it can be released via the urethra.*

Urethra *The urethra carries urine out of the body.*

Kidney *The kidneys are found at the back of the abdomen. The right one is lower than the left because it is underneath the liver.*

Medulla *The medulla contains tubules where water is reabsorbed and urine becomes more concentrated.*

Cortex *The cortex is found in the outer part of the kidney and contains glomeruli.*

LETTING GO

The bladder stores urine delivered from the kidneys. As it fills, stretch sensors in the bladder's muscular wall tell the brain it is time to go to the bathroom.

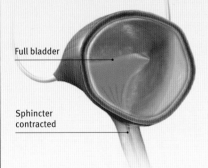

Full bladder

Sphincter contracted

When the sphincter muscle is contracted, urine is held within the bladder.

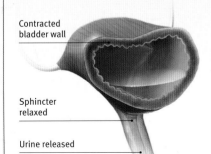

Contracted bladder wall

Sphincter relaxed

Urine released

When the sphincter muscle is relaxed and the bladder wall is contracted, urine is released.

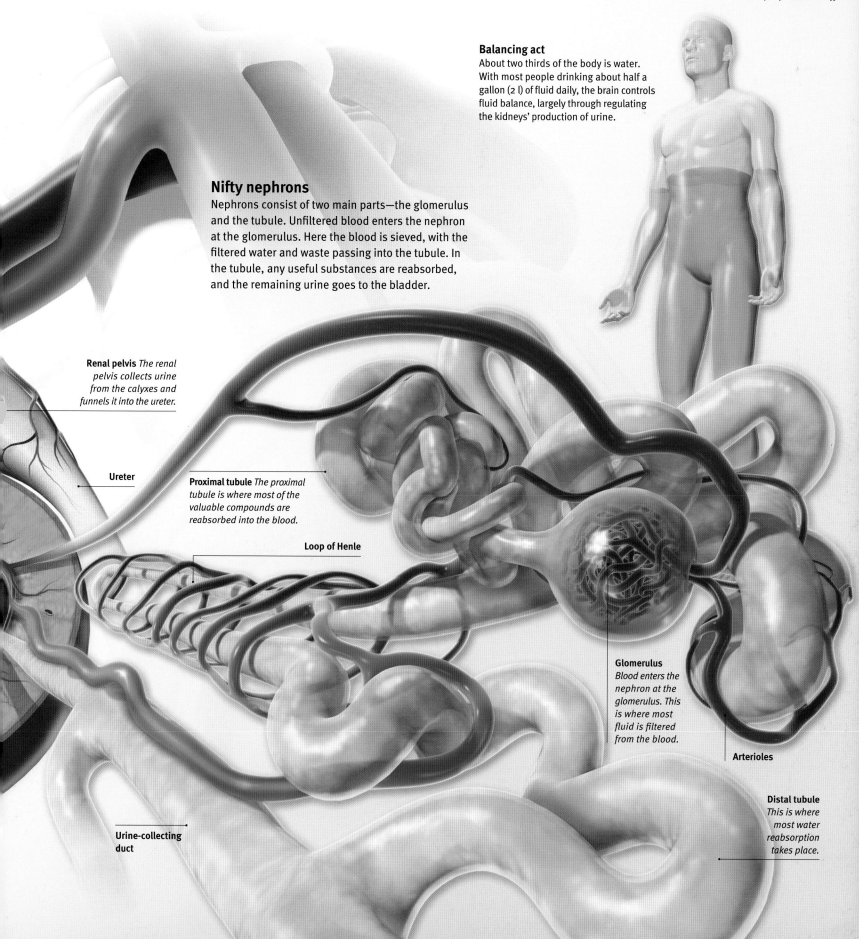

Balancing act

About two thirds of the body is water. With most people drinking about half a gallon (2 l) of fluid daily, the brain controls fluid balance, largely through regulating the kidneys' production of urine.

Nifty nephrons

Nephrons consist of two main parts—the glomerulus and the tubule. Unfiltered blood enters the nephron at the glomerulus. Here the blood is sieved, with the filtered water and waste passing into the tubule. In the tubule, any useful substances are reabsorbed, and the remaining urine goes to the bladder.

Renal pelvis *The renal pelvis collects urine from the calyxes and funnels it into the ureter.*

Ureter

Proximal tubule *The proximal tubule is where most of the valuable compounds are reabsorbed into the blood.*

Loop of Henle

Urine-collecting duct

Glomerulus *Blood enters the nephron at the glomerulus. This is where most fluid is filtered from the blood.*

Arterioles

Distal tubule *This is where most water reabsorption takes place.*

Reproduction

The reproductive system is dedicated to producing children and is different in men and women. Both must work together to make a baby, which requires the fusion of a single female sex cell with a single male sex cell. Women are born with all the female sex cells, or eggs, they will ever have. The eggs are stored in the two almond-shaped organs known as the ovaries, found in the pelvis. From about the age of eleven until about fifty, a woman will release one egg every month. Men, on the other hand, continuously produce millions of sex cells, known as sperm, daily from about the age of thirteen years.

Ovary Eggs are stored in the ovary, which also produces hormones that regulate pregnancy.

Uterus The uterus, or womb, is the organ in which a fetus develops during pregnancy.

Fimbriae These are finger-like projections that guide the egg into the fallopian tube.

Fallopian tube The egg travels from the ovary to the uterus through the fallopian tube.

Cervix The cervix is the lower end of the uterus, at the top of the vagina.

Bladder

Vagina The vagina connects the uterus to the outside of the body.

Female reproductive organs
Females have two ovaries, each connected to the uterus by a fallopian tube. The uterus is usually the size of a pear, but it expands enormously during pregnancy. The vagina links the uterus to the outside of the body.

Life begins

Sex cells contain only half the genetic material required to make a human being. When an egg is fertilized by a sperm, the resulting cell has a full set of genetic material, and an embryo begins to develop. Nine months after fertilization, the fully developed baby is ready to be born.

❷ **Cells divide** *After fertilization, the single cell divides into two. These two cells then divide into four, then eight, and so on. Within days there is a ball of dozens of dividing cells that embeds in the lining of the mother's womb.*

❶ **Sperm meets egg** *Despite hundreds of sperm cells gathering around the surface of an egg cell, only one will be used in the fertilization process. The single fertilized cell is smaller than the head of a pin.*

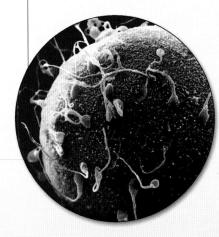

❸ **Body shaping** *At six weeks there are millions of dividing cells forming organs such as the brain, the liver, and the beating heart. The embryo is now the size of a grape and has arms, legs, ears, and eyes.*

④ Moving around *By three months the baby is about 2.5 inches (6 cm) long and is called a fetus. It moves its arms and legs within a sac containing watery amniotic fluid. Oxygen and nutrients are delivered to the fetus from the placenta via the umbilical cord.*

⑤ Ready for birth *At nine months, the fetus is now a baby ready to be born. The average weight of a baby at birth is about 7.5 pounds (3.4 kg), and the average length is 20 inches (50 cm).*

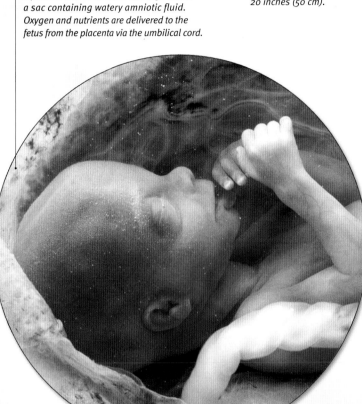

Two of a kind

Identical twins occur when a fertilized egg separates in two. Each half develops into a human being with identical genes. They look alike in every way. Non-identical, or fraternal, twins develop in the womb together, but from two fertilized eggs. They can look quite different from each other.

Male reproductive organs

Males have two testes and a penis, as well as a system of tubes and glands that connect them. Sperm are made and stored in the testes. After being mixed with semen from the seminal vesicles, the sperm are expelled from the urethra during ejaculation.

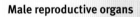

Penis The penis is the external male sex organ.

Urethra The urethra carries sperm and urine outside the body.

Testes These bean-shaped organs produce sperm.

Scrotum The scrotum is the "bag" that holds the testes outside the abdomen.

Bladder

Seminal vesicles Seminal vesicles produce the milky fluid known as semen.

Prostate The prostate is a walnut-size gland that surrounds the urethra.

Vas deferens The vas deferens transports the sperm toward the penis.

Epididymis The epididymis is the long, coiled tube where sperm mature.

SIGHT

SMELL

TASTE

HEARING

TOUCH

Sight

Sight is the most important sense in the body. It provides almost two-thirds of all the information that your brain processes. An eye works much like a nondigital camera. Light rays, reflected from objects, enter the eye through the clear, domed covering over the pupil, called the cornea. The light then passes through a lens, which, along with the cornea, focuses the rays as an upside-down image on the retina at the back of the eyeball. The retina has about 130 million cells that detect light and color, much like film in a camera. These cells generate electrical signals that travel via the optic nerve to the brain, where they are interpreted.

Seeing red
People with color-blindness often cannot tell the difference between red and green. It is a problem with the retina's color-sensitive cells, and it is more common in boys. If you are color-blind, you will not be able to see the number in this image (right).

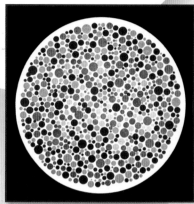

Lacrimal gland
The lacrimal gland produces tears.

Pupil

Iris

The pupil in bright light

Built-in sunglasses
In bright conditions, the iris shrinks the pupil to protect the retina. The pupil is dilated when more light is needed to see.

The pupil in normal light

The pupil in dim light

Tears

Nasolacrimal duct *This carries tear fluid into the nose.*

OUT OF FOCUS

A person will have problems focusing properly on objects if his or her eyeballs are an abnormal length. If the eye is too long, it will cause difficulties in seeing objects that are far away. This is called nearsightedness. Farsightedness is when the eye is too short, which makes it hard to see objects that are close-up. Glasses are the easiest way to rectify either problem.

Light work
The shape of the eyeball dictates where light hits the retina. If the eye is too long, the light focuses before the retina. If it is too short, the focal point will be past the retina.

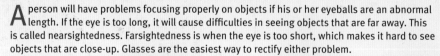

Nearsighted   Normal   Farsighted

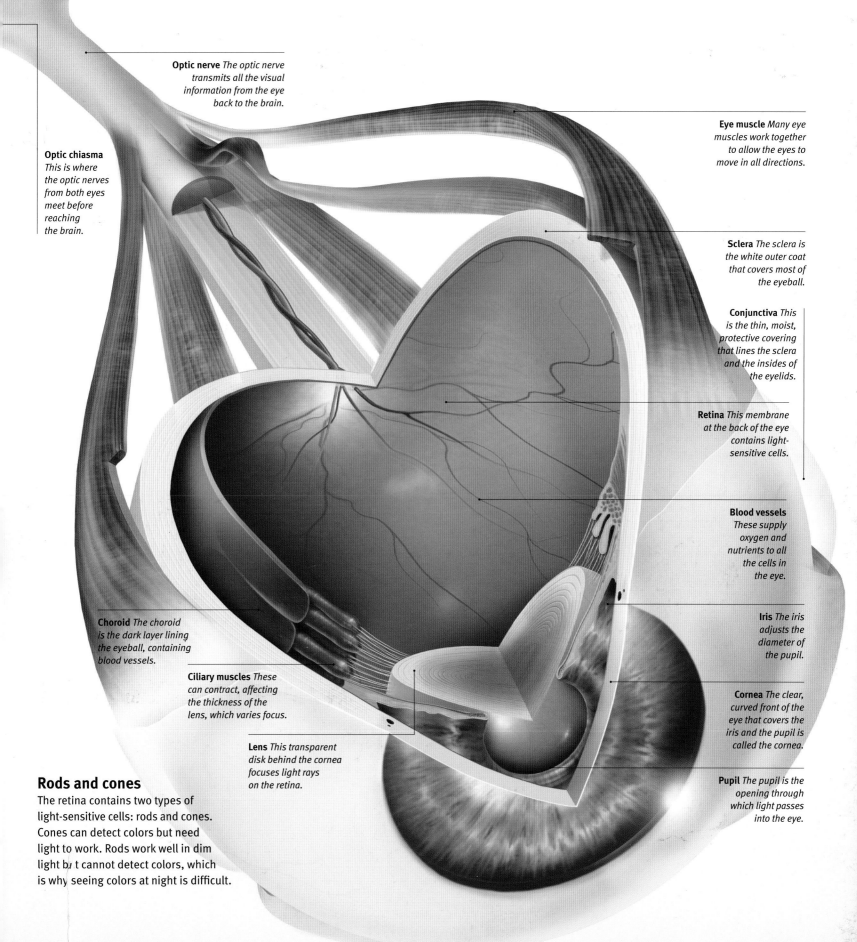

Optic nerve *The optic nerve transmits all the visual information from the eye back to the brain.*

Optic chiasma *This is where the optic nerves from both eyes meet before reaching the brain.*

Eye muscle *Many eye muscles work together to allow the eyes to move in all directions.*

Sclera *The sclera is the white outer coat that covers most of the eyeball.*

Conjunctiva *This is the thin, moist, protective covering that lines the sclera and the insides of the eyelids.*

Retina *This membrane at the back of the eye contains light-sensitive cells.*

Blood vessels *These supply oxygen and nutrients to all the cells in the eye.*

Choroid *The choroid is the dark layer lining the eyeball, containing blood vessels.*

Ciliary muscles *These can contract, affecting the thickness of the lens, which varies focus.*

Iris *The iris adjusts the diameter of the pupil.*

Cornea *The clear, curved front of the eye that covers the iris and the pupil is called the cornea.*

Lens *This transparent disk behind the cornea focuses light rays on the retina.*

Pupil *The pupil is the opening through which light passes into the eye.*

Rods and cones

The retina contains two types of light-sensitive cells: rods and cones. Cones can detect colors but need light to work. Rods work well in dim light but cannot detect colors, which is why seeing colors at night is difficult.

SIGHT

SMELL

TASTE

HEARING

TOUCH

Smell

Taste and smell work together, not only to help us enjoy food, but also to warn us if substances are possibly harmful. To fully experience a flavor, both senses need to be functioning, which is why food seems tasteless to a person with a cold. The sense of smell relies on odor receptors in the upper part of the nose. Odor molecules are breathed into the nose, where they come into contact with these receptors and generate electrical impulses. These are transmitted to the part of the brain that determines the nature of the smell, whether it is chocolate or rotten eggs. A person's nose can usually detect more than 10,000 different smells.

Scent sensors
Olfactory cells have hairs, called cilia, that detect passing scent molecules. These send information back to the brain via the olfactory bulb.

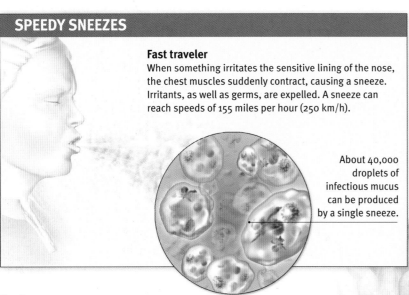

Nerves leading to brain

Receptor cells

Odor molecules

Olfactory cilia

SPEEDY SNEEZES

Fast traveler
When something irritates the sensitive lining of the nose, the chest muscles suddenly contract, causing a sneeze. Irritants, as well as germs, are expelled. A sneeze can reach speeds of 155 miles per hour (250 km/h).

About 40,000 droplets of infectious mucus can be produced by a single sneeze.

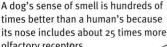

Dog's nose
A dog's sense of smell is hundreds of times better than a human's because its nose includes about 25 times more olfactory receptors.

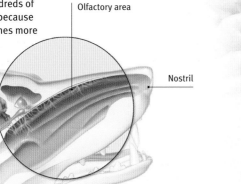

Olfactory area

Nostril

Olfactory bulb

Nostril

The nose knows
Olfactory areas are found on the roof of the nasal cavity. Each olfactory area contains about ten million odor-detecting cells.

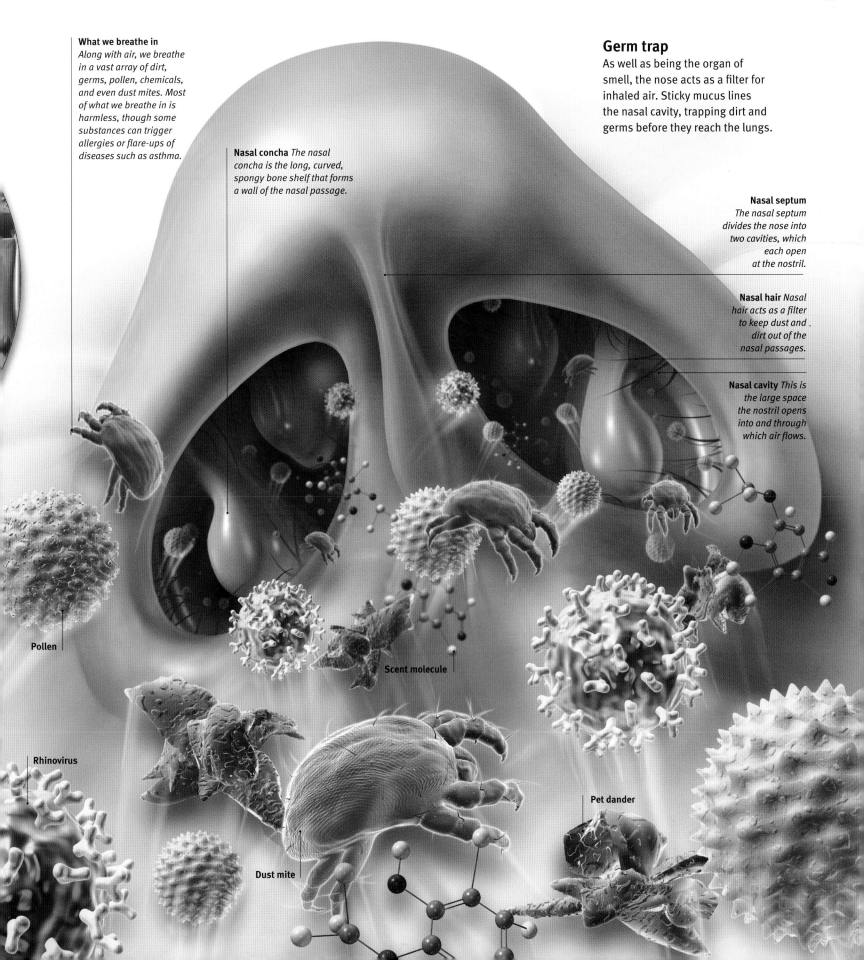

What we breathe in
Along with air, we breathe in a vast array of dirt, germs, pollen, chemicals, and even dust mites. Most of what we breathe in is harmless, though some substances can trigger allergies or flare-ups of diseases such as asthma.

Nasal concha *The nasal concha is the long, curved, spongy bone shelf that forms a wall of the nasal passage.*

Germ trap

As well as being the organ of smell, the nose acts as a filter for inhaled air. Sticky mucus lines the nasal cavity, trapping dirt and germs before they reach the lungs.

Nasal septum
The nasal septum divides the nose into two cavities, which each open at the nostril.

Nasal hair *Nasal hair acts as a filter to keep dust and dirt out of the nasal passages.*

Nasal cavity *This is the large space the nostril opens into and through which air flows.*

Pollen

Rhinovirus

Scent molecule

Pet dander

Dust mite

SIGHT

SMELL

TASTE

HEARING

TOUCH

Taste

Taste is the sense responsible for detecting flavor in food and drink. When food is eaten, flavors are dissolved in saliva, which makes them more likely to come in contact with the tongue's taste buds. More than eight thousand taste buds exist on the tongue's upper surface. Taste buds recognize only four basic tastes: salty, bitter, sour, and sweet. However, dozens of chemical-sensing cells in each taste bud send information about the proportions of the four basic tastes to the brain, to be interpreted as a unique flavor. The flavor-sensing cells in the taste buds are replaced every ten days.

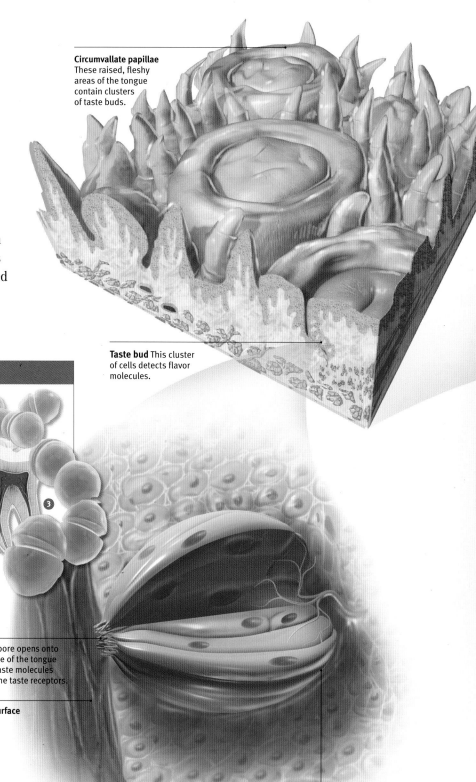

Circumvallate papillae These raised, fleshy areas of the tongue contain clusters of taste buds.

Taste bud This cluster of cells detects flavor molecules.

Pore The pore opens onto the surface of the tongue to allow taste molecules to reach the taste receptors.

Tongue surface

Taste cell This cell transmits taste information to the brain.

NOT SO SWEET

Sugar sticks to teeth and attracts bacteria that produce acid. This acid breaks down the hard surface of teeth and causes decay.

1. Decay begins on the surface of the tooth.
2. The decay reaches the dentin.
3. Finally, the decay hits the pulp, which contains sensitive nerves.

Salivary gland

Spit and polish
A person's three salivary glands make about 1.5 pints (710 ml) of saliva a day, which helps soften and digest food and keeps the mouth clean.

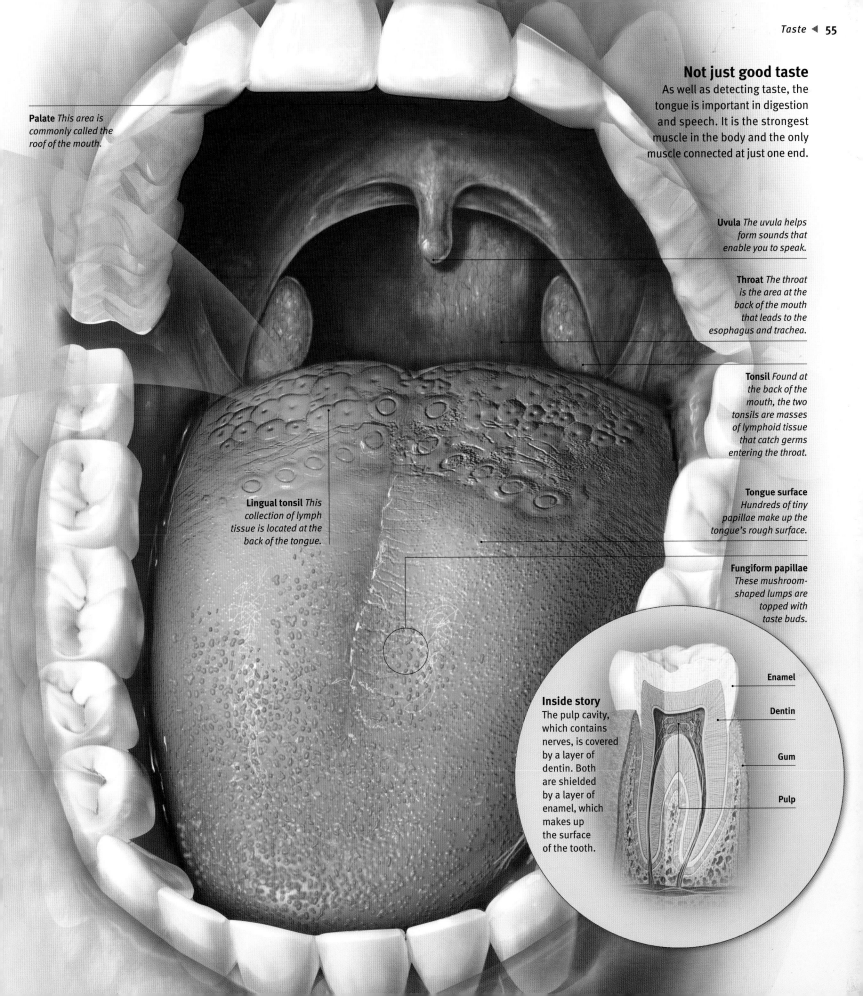

Palate *This area is commonly called the roof of the mouth.*

Not just good taste

As well as detecting taste, the tongue is important in digestion and speech. It is the strongest muscle in the body and the only muscle connected at just one end.

Uvula *The uvula helps form sounds that enable you to speak.*

Throat *The throat is the area at the back of the mouth that leads to the esophagus and trachea.*

Tonsil *Found at the back of the mouth, the two tonsils are masses of lymphoid tissue that catch germs entering the throat.*

Lingual tonsil *This collection of lymph tissue is located at the back of the tongue.*

Tongue surface *Hundreds of tiny papillae make up the tongue's rough surface.*

Fungiform papillae *These mushroom-shaped lumps are topped with taste buds.*

Inside story
The pulp cavity, which contains nerves, is covered by a layer of dentin. Both are shielded by a layer of enamel, which makes up the surface of the tooth.

Enamel

Dentin

Gum

Pulp

SIGHT
SMELL
TASTE
HEARING
TOUCH

Hearing

Hearing involves registering sounds from the outside world and transmitting them to the brain so they can be interpreted. Sound travels in waves. These waves move down the ear canal until they hit the eardrum, causing the thin membrane of the eardrum to vibrate. This sets off a chain reaction of vibration down three tiny bones to the fluid-filled inner ear. The vibrations create ripples in the fluid. When the microscopic hairs in the inner ear detect movement in the fluid, they transmit signals along the nerves to the brain, which can then interpret the signals as sounds.

Helix

Triangular fossa

Pinna

Anti-helix

Concha

Intertragic notch

Lobule

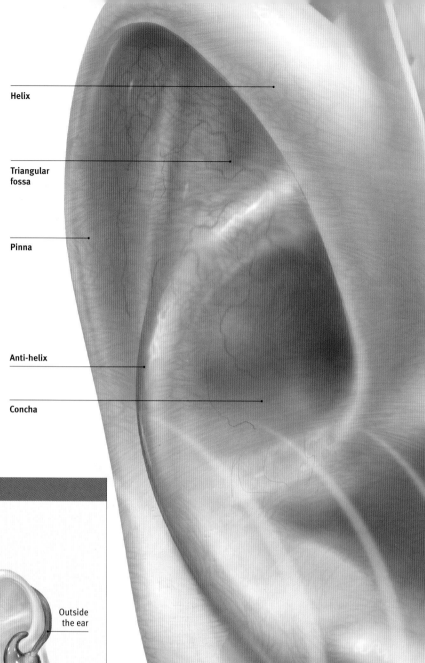

HARD OF HEARING

Poor hearing, or hearing loss, can be caused by many factors. Sometimes genetic disorders passed down through a family cause hearing loss or damage. Continual exposure to loud noises can also be a cause of hearing impairment later in life.

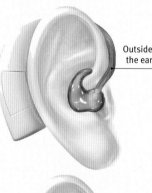

Outside the ear

Inside the ear

Aids for hearing
Poor hearing is sometimes helped by hearing aids. These are electronic devices that receive sound through a microphone, then amplify it before transmitting it to the eardrum. The devices can sit inside or outside the ear.

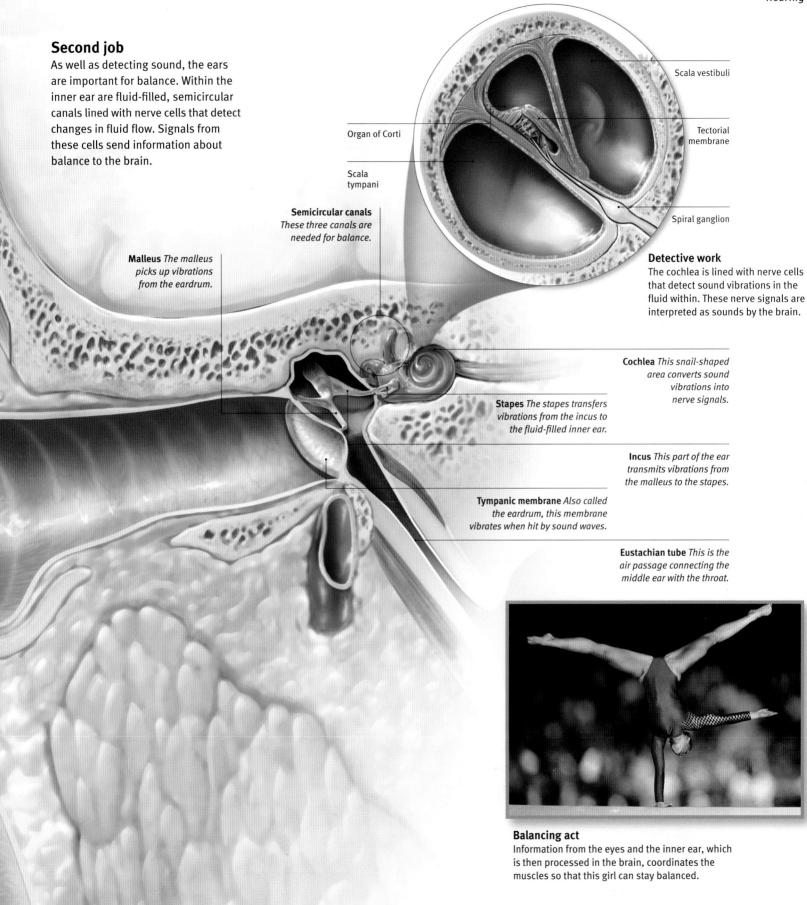

Second job

As well as detecting sound, the ears are important for balance. Within the inner ear are fluid-filled, semicircular canals lined with nerve cells that detect changes in fluid flow. Signals from these cells send information about balance to the brain.

Scala vestibuli

Organ of Corti

Tectorial membrane

Scala tympani

Spiral ganglion

Semicircular canals *These three canals are needed for balance.*

Malleus *The malleus picks up vibrations from the eardrum.*

Detective work
The cochlea is lined with nerve cells that detect sound vibrations in the fluid within. These nerve signals are interpreted as sounds by the brain.

Cochlea *This snail-shaped area converts sound vibrations into nerve signals.*

Stapes *The stapes transfers vibrations from the incus to the fluid-filled inner ear.*

Incus *This part of the ear transmits vibrations from the malleus to the stapes.*

Tympanic membrane *Also called the eardrum, this membrane vibrates when hit by sound waves.*

Eustachian tube *This is the air passage connecting the middle ear with the throat.*

Balancing act
Information from the eyes and the inner ear, which is then processed in the brain, coordinates the muscles so that this girl can stay balanced.

SIGHT

SMELL

TASTE

HEARING

TOUCH

Touch

The sense of touch is managed through receptors in the skin—the body's largest sensory organ. Millions of nerve cells distributed throughout the skin register pressure, pain, heat, cold, and touch. The sensitivity of a particular part of the body is determined by the number of sensory receptors on its surface. The most sensitive areas of the body are the hands, lips, face, tongue, and fingertips. The least sensitive area is the middle of the back. Nerve signals from sensory receptors are sent to the brain and interpreted in the region known as the touch center, or sensory cortex.

Staying in touch
The blue strip on the brain to the right shows the location of the brain's touch center. It is divided into sections that process touch information from various parts of the body, as illustrated below.

Touch center

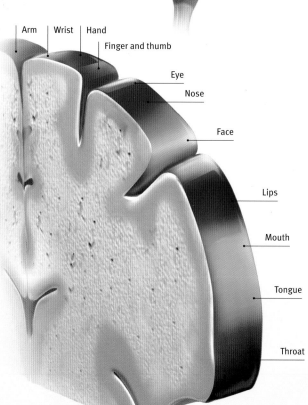

Arm | Wrist | Hand
Finger and thumb
Eye
Nose
Face
Lips
Mouth
Tongue
Throat

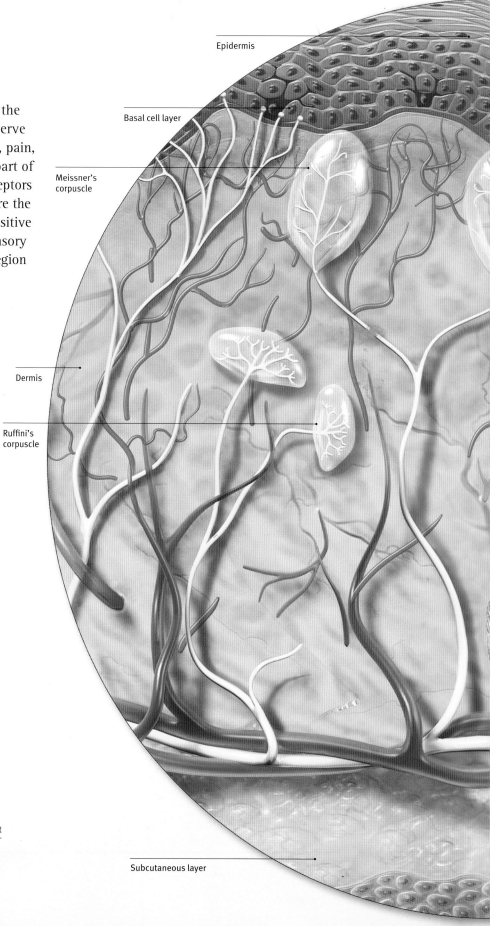

Epidermis

Basal cell layer

Meissner's corpuscle

Dermis

Ruffini's corpuscle

Subcutaneous layer

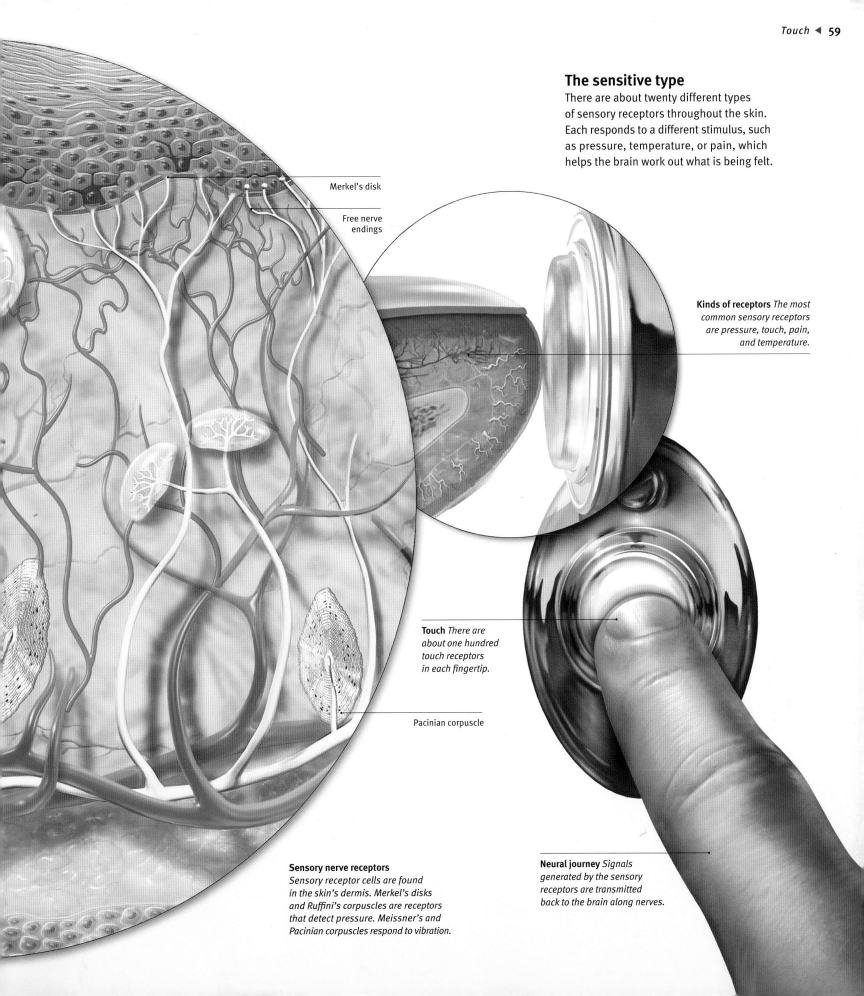

The sensitive type

There are about twenty different types of sensory receptors throughout the skin. Each responds to a different stimulus, such as pressure, temperature, or pain, which helps the brain work out what is being felt.

Merkel's disk

Free nerve endings

Kinds of receptors *The most common sensory receptors are pressure, touch, pain, and temperature.*

Touch *There are about one hundred touch receptors in each fingertip.*

Pacinian corpuscle

Sensory nerve receptors
Sensory receptor cells are found in the skin's dermis. Merkel's disks and Ruffini's corpuscles are receptors that detect pressure. Meissner's and Pacinian corpuscles respond to vibration.

Neural journey *Signals generated by the sensory receptors are transmitted back to the brain along nerves.*

Body File

Good balance

A healthy, balanced diet is the most important way to maintain good health. This food pyramid is an effective guide to the proportion of different food groups that you should eat each day.

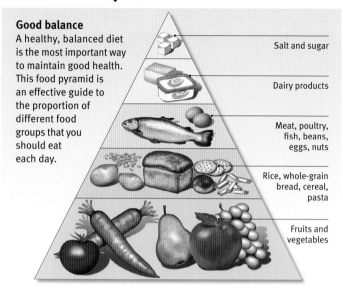

Salt and sugar

Dairy products

Meat, poultry, fish, beans, eggs, nuts

Rice, whole-grain bread, cereal, pasta

Fruits and vegetables

WORLD OF ENERGY

World diet

A calorie (kilojoule) is a unit of energy that measures the energy content of food. The average recommended amount of calories to consume each day is 2,000 (8,400 kj) for women and 2,500 (10,000 kj) for men. The map below shows the different amounts of calories consumed each day by people from different countries in the world.

■ More than 3,200 calories (13,400 kilojoules) per person
■ 2,900–3,200 calories (12,000–13,400 kilojoules) per person
■ 2,600–2,900 calories (10,900–12,000 kilojoules) per person
■ 2,300–2,600 calories (9,600–10,900 kilojoules) per person
■ 2,000–2,300 calories (8,400–9,600 kilojoules) per person
■ Fewer than 2,000 calories (8,400 kilojoules) per person
□ Insufficient data

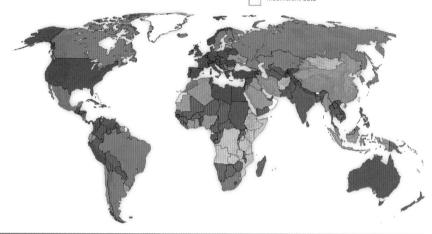

VITAMIN AND MINERAL GUIDE

Vitamin	Good sources	Main functions
A	Meat, dairy, vegetables	Helps vision, defends against infections, and maintains skin, hair, and nails.
D	Fish-liver oils, egg yolks, fortified milk; also formed in the skin when exposed to sunlight	Maintains normal blood levels of calcium.
E	Whole grains, leafy green vegetables, vegetable oils, egg yolks	Antioxidant that helps stop cell damage.
K	Made by microorganisms in the gut	Needed for blood clotting.
B1 (thiamine)	Lean meat, enriched cereals, nuts, yeast products	Helps process carbohydrates and is involved in nerve and heart function.
B2 (riboflavin)	Milk and milk products, enriched cereals, meat, eggs, yeast products	Helps process carbohydrates, repair tissue, and maintain mucous membranes.
Niacin	Yeast products, milk, meat, fish, poultry, legumes, eggs, whole-grain cereals	Needed for processing carbohydrates and for energy.
B6	Fish, legumes, whole-grain cereals, meat, potatoes, eggs	Needed for processing amino acids and fatty acids; helps the nervous system function.
Pantothenic acid	Most foods—especially liver, yeast products, egg yolks	Helps release energy from carbohydrates, fats, and protein.
Folate (folic acid)	Leafy green vegetables, organ meats, whole grains, legumes	Helps the body create new cells.
B12	Most animal products	Important for function of cells and red blood cell production.

Vitamin	Good sources	Main functions
Biotin	Made by microorganisms in the gut; also found in liver, egg yolks, legumes	Helps the body process carbohydrates and fatty acids.
C (ascorbic acid)	Citrus fruits, berries, peppers, cantaloupe, cabbage, cauliflower, broccoli	Tissue growth and wound repair, maintains the health of cells, plays a role in brain and nerve function.

Mineral	Good sources	Main functions
Calcium	Milk and milk products, canned fish with bones, tofu, dark green vegetables, molasses	Aids the growth of bones and teeth. Also needed for nerve and muscle function.
Fluorine	Fluoridated water	Needed for bone and tooth growth.
Iodine	Seafood, iodized salt	Formation of thyroid hormones.
Iron	Meat (especially red meat), liver, whole grains, leafy green vegetables, tofu, egg yolks	Main component of red blood cells and muscle cells. Also helps the formation of enzymes.
Magnesium	Legumes, dark green vegetables, nuts, whole-grain cereals	Needed for bone and tooth growth and nerve and muscle function.
Phosphorus	Meat, poultry, whole-grain cereals	Helps bone and tooth growth.
Potassium	Milk, bananas	Needed for nerve and muscle function.
Selenium	Meat, wheatgerm, seafood	Used by the body as an antioxidant.
Sodium	Salt, most processed foods	Aids nerve and muscle function.
Zinc	Meat, eggs, dairy products	Used for wound repair, body growth, and for taste and smell.

Game of chance

Where you live in the world can play a major role in your health and the length of your life. Access to clean water, nutritious food, and medical care all affect our risk of disease and how long we live.

- Infectious and parasitic diseases
- Cancers
- Cardiovascular diseases
- Childbirth-related illness
- Injuries
- Other*

*Other causes of death include nutritional deficiencies, nervous disorders, diabetes, cirrhosis of the liver, pulmonary disease, kidney conditions, and birth defects.

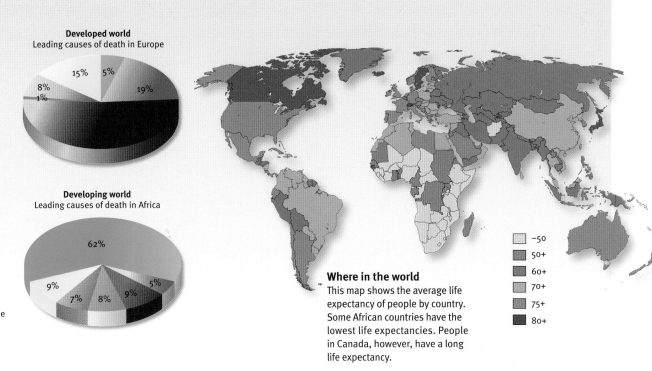

Developed world
Leading causes of death in Europe

15% · 5% · 8% · 1% · 19%

Developing world
Leading causes of death in Africa

62% · 9% · 7% · 8% · 9% · 5%

Where in the world
This map shows the average life expectancy of people by country. Some African countries have the lowest life expectancies. People in Canada, however, have a long life expectancy.

- −50
- 50+
- 60+
- 70+
- 75+
- 80+

BODY SYSTEMS AT A GLANCE

System	System parts	Main functions
Nervous	Brain, spinal cord, nerves	Senses external and internal stimuli; controls and coordinates all body systems; source of thought, memory, and emotion.
Endocrine	Glands, including pituitary, thyroid, pancreas, testes, ovaries	Releases hormones that control and regulate body functions.
Reproductive	Female: ovaries, fallopian tubes, uterus, vagina	Female: produces eggs; nurtures developing fetus; coordinates childbirth.
	Male: testes, sperm ducts, seminal vessels, penis	Male: produces sperm, allows fertilization.
Digestive	Mouth, esophagus, stomach, intestines, liver, pancreas, gall bladder	Absorbs nutrients from ingested foods, then makes them available to body cells; eliminates waste.
Respiratory	Trachea, bronchi, lungs, diaphragm	Takes in oxygen and delivers it to body cells; removes carbon dioxide.
Circulatory	Heart, blood vessels	Transports oxygen, carbon dioxide, nutrients, and hormones around the body; helps regulate body temperature.
Lymphatic	Lymph, lymph vessels, lymph nodes, spleen	Collects and returns fluids to the blood; helps defend the body against infection and tissue damage.
Urinary	Kidneys, bladder, ureter, urethra	Controls and maintains tissue fluids; excretes waste products.

Heart

Stomach

Muscle

Tendon

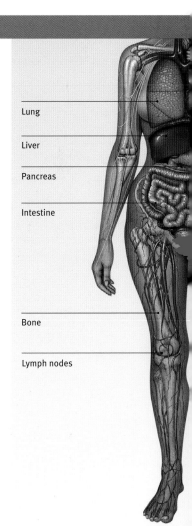

Lung

Liver

Pancreas

Intestine

Bone

Lymph nodes

Glossary

alveoli Tiny air sacs found in the lung, where oxygen inhaled during breathing is absorbed into the bloodstream.

artery A blood vessel that usually carries oxygen-rich blood away from the heart.

asthma A disease where a trigger causes narrowing of the airways, making breathing difficult and leading to symptoms such as coughing and wheezing.

atrium One of the two small upper chambers of the heart that receives blood from veins.

axon The long extension of the nerve cell that carries electrical impulses away from the body of the neuron.

bronchus One of two main airways branching from the trachea that delivers air to and from the lungs.

cerebellum The part of the brain that controls balance and coordination.

chromosome The X-shaped structure inside a cell that contains genetic information.

cilia Tiny, hairlike projections that help propel fluid over body surfaces.

clavicle The bone that connects the shoulder to the sternum. Also known as the collarbone.

cochlea The part of the inner ear that is essential for hearing.

compact bone The hard, dense, outer layer of bones that gives them strength.

cone cells In the retina, cone cells detect color.

conjunctiva The moist, slippery membrane that covers the eyeball and the inside of the eyelids.

corpus callosum The arched band of nerve tissue within the brain that connects the two hemispheres.

cranium The dome-shaped bone that covers and protects the brain.

CT scan An imaging technique that uses X-rays to provide information that, when processed by a computer, produces pictures of tissues and organs within the body.

dendrite The shorter projection on a nerve cell that carries electrical impulses toward the body of the neuron.

dermis The inner layer of skin that contains the blood vessels, nerve cells, sweat glands, and hair roots.

diaphragm The curved sheet of muscle that separates the chest cavity from the abdomen.

diastole The period of time in which the heart fills with blood.

DNA (deoxyribonucleic acid) The chemical that makes up chromosomes and carries genes. This is found within the nucleus of the cell.

embryo A newly developing animal within the womb. Developing human babies are known as embryos from three to eight weeks after fertilization.

epidermis The tough outer layer of skin, where dead cells are constantly being shed and replaced by new cells.

epididymus A long, coiled tube found behind the testicle, where sperm mature and are stored.

epiglottis An elastic flap of tissue found in the larynx, which covers the trachea when eating; this prevents food and liquid from entering the lungs.

erythrocyte Also known as a red blood cell, this contains the pigment hemoglobin, which carries oxygen needed by most tissues in the body.

esophagus The muscular tube that propels food down to the stomach from the mouth.

eustachian tube The bony passageway within the skull that links the middle ear with the back of the throat. This is used for pressure equalization.

fetus An unborn animal in the later development stages within the womb. Developing human babies are known as fetuses from eight weeks after fertilization until birth.

gland A tissue or organ that produces a substance, such as saliva or a hormone, which it releases into the body.

hemoglobin The pigment found in red blood cells, to which oxygen binds.

hormone A substance released into the blood by an endocrine gland. This substance causes a specific reaction in cells.

humerus The bone found in the upper arm, linking the shoulder to the elbow.

immune system The body's defense system. It consists of white blood cells that protect against invading germs.

incus One of the three small bones found in the middle ear. It helps transmit sound to the inner ear.

interossei The collective name given to the small muscles of the hand.

intestinal villi Tiny, finger-like projections in the small bowel. These increase surface area and aid in the absorption of nutrients from food.

keratin A tough body protein that is a major component of hair and nails.

larynx The part of the respiratory system between the pharynx and the trachea, which contains the vocal cords.

lymph A straw-colored liquid that is collected from body tissues and flows through the lymphatic vessels. It contains water, protein, and white blood cells.

lymphocyte A type of white blood cell that plays an important part in the body's immune system.

lymph node A bean-shaped mass of lymph tissue.

macrophage A type of white blood cell that destroys invading germs or dead cells.

malleus One of the three tiny bones of the middle ear that transmit sound. Also known as the hammer because of its shape.

mandible The movable lower jawbone, which is attached by a ball and socket joint to the rest of the skull.

maxilla The immovable upper jawbone, which forms the wall of the cheek.

medulla In bones, the medulla is the bone marrow. In the brain, the medulla forms part of the brain stem. Its major role is to control involuntary functions such as breathing.

medullary cavity The cavity in bones where bone marrow can be found.

melanin A brown to black pigment found naturally in human skin and hair.

mitosis The process where a cell divides in half, forming an identical replica of itself.

MRI An imaging technique that uses magnetic fields and radio waves to gather information. The information is processed by a computer to generate images of the inside of the body.

nephron One of about a million microscopic blood-filtering units found in the kidney.

neuron A nerve cell that transmits electrical impulses along its long projections.

nucleus In cells, the nucleus is the control center. It contains all the genetic material that dictates the cell's function.

olfactory area An area within the nasal cavity where smells are detected by special cells.

patella This is found in the quadriceps tendon at the front of the knee. Also known as the kneecap.

pathogen A disease-causing microscopic organism such as a virus or bacteria.

pinna The part of the ear that projects out from the head.

pituitary gland A small gland found in the brain, which has a role in controlling growth

platelet A cell found in blood that sticks to other platelets to help form a clot, which stops bleeding.

pons A component of the brain stem found at the base of the brain.

prostate A gland found in men that surrounds the urethra at the base of the bladder.

radius The shorter of the two forearm bones, connecting the elbow to the wrist.

retina The light-sensitive area at the back of the eyeball.

rod A light-sensitive cell found in the retina.

sacrum A curved, triangular bone found in the pelvis at the base of the spine.

sartorius The longest muscle in the body. It is found in the upper leg.

scapula Also known as the shoulder blade, this triangular bone found on the upper back forms part of the shoulder joint.

semicircular canal One of three fluid-filled cavities that forms part of the inner ear and maintains balance.

spleen The largest lymphatic organ in the body.

stapes The smallest bone in the body. One of the three small bones found in the middle ear. Also known as the stirrup because of its shape.

synapse The junction between nerve cells. Electrical impulses are transmitted across a synapse by means of chemicals known as neurotransmitters.

systole The period of time in which the heart contracts, forcing blood out into the arteries.

thoracic duct The vessel into which the largest lymphatic vessels drain before the lymph is deposited into the bloodstream.

trachea The tube extending from the pharynx to the bronchi, through which air travels to and from the lungs. Also known as the windpipe.

tympanic membrane Also known as the eardrum, this is the taut membrane that separates the outer ear from the middle ear. The tympanic membrane vibrates in response to sound.

ulna The longer of the two bones found in the forearm.

ultrasound A means of scanning, where high-pitched sound waves are directed to the body and the echoes created are recorded and interpreted.

uterus The organ in women in which a fertilized egg develops into a baby over a period of 40 weeks. Also known as the womb.

vas deferens The tube through which sperm is transported from the testes to the urethra.

ventricle In the heart, one of two thick-walled lower chambers from which blood is pumped to either the lungs or the rest of the body.

X-ray Invisible rays that pass through most body tissues but cannot penetrate bone or metal.

Index

Credits

The publisher thanks Alexandra Cooper and Megan Schwenke
for their contributions, and Puddingburn for the index.

ILLUSTRATIONS

Illustrations by Argosy Publishing, www.argosypublishing.com,
with the exception of some additional illustrations:
12–13 **Susanna Addario; Tony Gibbons/Bernard Thornton Artists UK;**
Moonrunner Design; Claudia Saraceni
26–27 **John Bull; Christer Eriksson (main image)**
60–61 **Peter Bull Art Studio; Trevor Ruth**

PHOTOGRAPHS

Key t=top; l=left; r=right; tl=top left; tcl=top center left; tc=top center;
tcr=top center right; tr=top right; cl=center left; c=center; cr=center
right; b=bottom; bl=bottom left; bcl=bottom center left; bc=bottom
center; bcr=bottom center right; br=bottom right

APL=Australian Picture Library; APL/CBT=Australian Picture Library/
Corbis; GI=Getty Images; iS=istockphoto.com; PL=photolibrary.com

1b PL; 4bl PL; 8bl, tr PL; 12bl, br, c, cr, tr PL; c Chris Shorten; tr APL; 13bl,
c, r, t, tc, tl PL; br APL; t iS; 16cr PL; 17bl, tr PL; br iS; 20tr PL; 24c APL; tr
PL; 30br APL; 32bl PL; 36bl PL; bl iS; 43tl PL; 44tr PL; 48c, l, r PL; 49l, r
PL; 50tr PL; 56bl PL; 57br APL/CBT

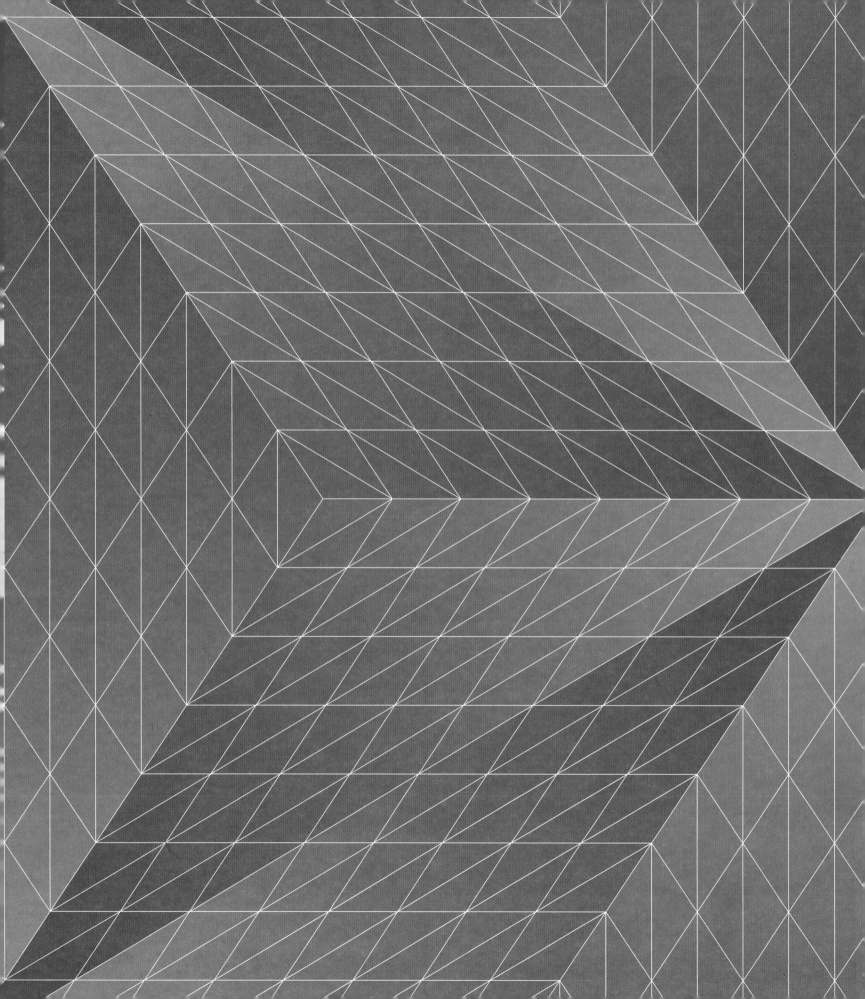